COMING OF AGE IN WAR-TORN LITHUANIA AND GERMANY

GEORGE P. BLUM

 www.trafford.com
North America & international
toll-free: 844-688-6899 (USA & Canada)
fax: 812 355 4082

For Barbara and Alfred

Acknowledgements

My friend Mike Sharp, who until his recent retirement taught German language and literature at the University of the Pacific, has heard me talk about some of my experiences related in these reminiscences in our frequent conversations about German affairs. He read the manuscript before it reached the final stages and raised a number of helpful queries that improved its content. I am indebted to Julienne Hastings, my daughter-in-law, for translating my suggestions into an exquisite cover design. My foremost debt is owed to my wife, Beverly, who carefully edited the manuscript. She has provided support and encouragement in the writing of my recollections throughout the years and also suggested the title for this memoir. Whatever errors in fact, interpretation, and formulation remain are all mine.

Contents

Chronology

1731-32	Salzburg Protestants expelled and many moved to East Prussia.
1772, 1793, 1795	Partitions of Poland.
Around 1800	Some of my paternal Salzburg ancestors migrated from East Prussia to Lithuania.
1914-18	World War I.
1923	Lithuania annexed the Memel region.
March 1939	Hitler seized the Memel (Klaipeda) region from Lithuania.
August 1939	Nazi-Soviet Pact.
1940-41	First Soviet occupation of Lithuania.
1939-45	World War II.
Early 1941	Resettlement of the Germans from Lithuania.
1941-44	German occupation of Lithuania.
Late 1942-43	Many Germans from Lithuania returned to their homeland.
Summer of 1944	Germans evacuated from Lithuania when the Red Army advanced and reoccupied Lithuania.
Late 1944 – May 1945	Soviet armies conquered eastern and central Germany.
1946-1947	Expulsion of Germans from areas east of the Oder-Neisse line.

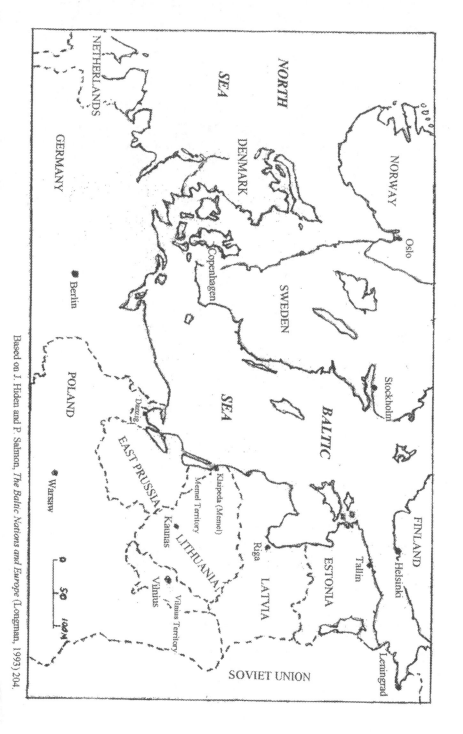

Interwar Baltic Region

Map 1

Based on J. Hiden and P. Salmon, *The Baltic Nations and Europe* (Longman, 1993) 204.

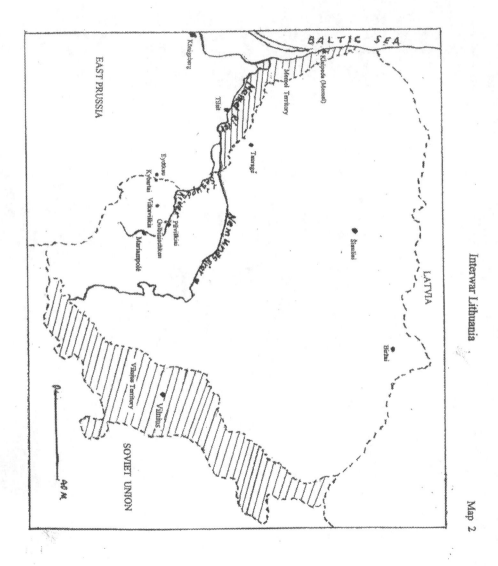

Interwar Lithuania

Map 2

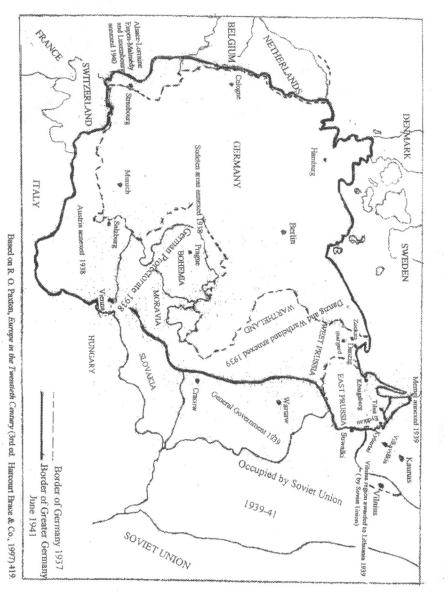

Interwar Germany until 1937 and Greater Germany June 1941   Map 3

FRANCE

SWITZERLAND

ITALY

Alsace-Lorraine
Eupen-Malmédy
and Luxembourg
annexed 1940

Strasbourg

BELGIUM

NETHERLANDS

Cologne

GERMANY

Munich

Salzburg

Austria annexed 1938

Sudeten areas annexed 1938

German Protectorate 1938

BOHEMIA

Prague

MORAVIA

Vienna

HUNGARY

SLOVAKIA

Hamburg

Berlin

Danzig and Wartheland annexed 1939

WARTHELAND

WEST PRUSSIA

Zichenau
Danzig
Königsberg

EAST PRUSSIA

Suvalki

DENMARK

SWEDEN

Memel annexed 1939

Tilsit

Vilna region
Vilnius region awarded to Lithuania 1939
(by Soviet Union)

Vilna/Vilnius

Kaunas

Cracow

Warsaw

General Government 1939

Occupied by Soviet Union

1939–41

SOVIET UNION

- - - - - - Border of Germany 1937
————— Border of Greater Germany
June 1941

Based on R. O. Paxton, Europe in the Twentieth Century (3rd ed. Harcourt Brace & Co., 1997) 419.

Map 4

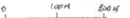

East and West Germany 1945-1990

Based on D. Orlow, *A History of Modern Germany*
(5th ed. Prentice Hall, 2002) 231.
With some additions.

Introduction

One day in the summer of 1940 I watched with astonishment if not some trepidation a troop of Russian soldiers moving right by the house on the street in Pilviškiai, Lithuania, where my parents and I then lived. The outward appearance of the Russian military men was not impressive, for many of them wore rather shabby gray brown uniforms and rode in downright primitive horse-drawn carts. They were probably on their way to new military bases or on maneuver. As an eight-year-old, I strikingly sensed that unexpected changes were happening around me and they were not changes for the better. From conversations of my parents with relatives and friends that I overheard, I knew that Germany was at war with Britain after having defeated and occupied Poland in early fall 1939 and then France in late spring 1940; and now I saw Soviet troops who looked like aliens to me occupying the very region of Lithuania where I lived. The vivid memory of this childhood event has remained with me and relates very much to the experiences of the first twenty years of my life, which I spent in Lithuania and Germany. I decided rather late in my career in 1999, after retiring from four decades of teaching modern European and German history in college, to write an autobiographical narrative of experiences that preceded and followed what I had observed on that summer day of 1940. It is my personal family life story embedded in the unsettled years of prewar and immediate postwar history of Lithuania and Germany.

While teaching I had paid little attention to my family's history or even learned much about the diverse past of the Baltic States. Once I decided to relate some, to me, notable episodes from my early life in a memoir, I could no longer query my father and mother or an uncle and several aunts about some of the details of our family's past that might have helped me to sketch a fuller picture. All these close family members of my parents' generation had passed on years before I started thinking seriously about family history. In several instances, some of my German cousins were able to answer questions about their parents' lives during the times when we all were growing up. The documents that survive from the past of my family include some well-worn birth and marriage certificates or certified copies, a number of letters that contain early family reminiscences, notes with dates of events that I kept as a young teenager after the war, and, quite importantly, numerous family photographs. Several sporadic church publications from my father's time of service in the Baltic Methodist church have also helped to complement what I remembered from my parents' conversations over the years.

For the family history on my father's side, a compilation of stories that my German cousin Arkadius Blum collected and edited from the contributions of relatives in Germany and outside Germany about their lives was particularly valuable. This family history book was published in German in 1983. It contains personal narratives related by different relatives of their experiences during the prewar and war years, their resettlement to Germany, and the flight from Lithuania and eastern Germany, often illustrated with some photographs. The fairly widespread readership of this family history book included relatives in Germany, the United States, Canada, Brazil, and Australia. During World War II and on one or two occasions after the war, Arkadius was able to examine some church registers in the Salzburg region of Austria and confirm much of the oral tradition passed on through generations about the early origins of my paternal ancestors who were expelled from there in the 1700s and migrated to East Prussia. As much as I have learned, no church register records relating to the sites where my ancestors lived in Lithuania, once part of the Russian Tsarist Empire, survived the resettlement of the Germans from Lithuania in 1941 and the Soviet occupations (1940-1941, 1944-1991). Lastly, I have also drawn on historical monographs and accounts, as indicated in the narrative, to sketch some of the larger historical developments that impinged on my family's life.

I was persuaded to attempt this personal memoir by members of my family and some friends who encouraged me to write down what I had lived through and experienced in the turmoil of Europe before immigrating to the United States as a young adult. Writing this memoir has enabled me to understand better how many of the events that my parents and I experienced in the prelude to World War II, during the turbulent years of the war, and during its painful and unsettling aftermath had been determined or shaped by decision makers and governments at a level of which my family and I were only vaguely aware at the time. Certainly the provisions of the Nazi-Soviet Pact of 1939, the postwar settlements of WW II, and the amended US Displaced Persons Act of 1950 had a decisive impact on the direction of my life and my parents' lives.

My father was a third-generation ethnic German in Lithuania. When he was born in 1890, his land of birth was incorporated into the Russian Empire, which made him a subject of the Russian tsar. My mother was born in 1898, grew up in East Prussia, Germany, and migrated to Lithuania after World War I when she was in her late twenties.

My father spoke German as his native language and gained the mastery of Russian in school. He also learned to speak Lithuanian well in the 1920s after Lithuania had become an independent state, as did my mother when she moved to Lithuania in the mid-1920s. I myself did not learn Lithuanian until I started elementary school. Perhaps not surprisingly, I have never considered Lithuania my homeland even though I was born there and lived there during my early childhood, albeit in a somewhat sheltered German-speaking family who identified with German culture and the German language.

My early childhood neighborhood however was multiethnic and multicultural. On one side of the street of my parents' home in the small Lithuanian town where we lived between 1935 and 1941 were Lithuanian neighbors; on the other side, only a house down or two, was a Lithuanian Catholic elementary and early secondary school, and diagonally across from us were more Lithuanian and some Jewish neighbors. Since I did not speak Lithuanian in my early boyhood, I had little contact with children other than Germans, mostly first and second cousins living half a mile or more away from my home. The only non-German people that I could understand somewhat before learning Lithuanian were Jews who spoke Yiddish, which grew out of medieval German dialects but is written in Hebrew characters. It was commonly spoken among Lithuanian and Eastern European Jews.

Before proceeding with my family's history and my own recollections, I will sketch Lithuanian history, the multifaceted life of the German minority in Lithuania, their religious heritage and culture, and, in my family's case, the small Methodist minority in the Baltic region. This discussion will place my family's history in its broader European social and cultural context

Historical and Social Background

Lithuania's Difficult Path through the Centuries

Lithuania is the largest of the three Baltic States with an area the size of West Virginia. At the end of 1939, Lithuania held around 2.9 million people, including the recently restored historic and cultural capital of Vilnius, while Latvia and Estonia, its northern neighbors, had a combined population not much larger than that of Lithuania. In my early boyhood years, many Lithuanians exhibited an intense nationalistic attitude, since their homeland had only recently regained its independence in 1918, at the end of World War I, after centuries of oppressive foreign rule. Lithuania was the least developed of the new Baltic States but it drew upon its renowned medieval past for inspiration to create its modern national identity and statehood. As a young boy I was quite aware how the Lithuanian government tried to capture and celebrate its land's historic "greatness" in the 13th and 14th centuries through monuments of medieval rulers, patriotic stamps, nationalistic publications, and the teaching of public spirited history lessons in schools.

It was around 1230 that the Lithuanian Grand Duke Mindaugas managed to unify the Lithuanian tribes into a single state. Two decades later he was crowned King of Lithuania, but was to remain the first and only ruler to obtain that title. In the following century, Lithuanian grand dukes became aggressive conquerors and expanded their dominion over areas that today comprise Belarus and Ukraine. They also embraced the Catholic faith and formed a personal union with Poland largely to fend off the threat of the German Teutonic Order of Knights, who lorded over modern day western Poland, the Russian region of today's Kaliningrad (before 1945 Königsberg and

East Prussia), Latvia, and Estonia. Under Grand Duke Vytautas the Great the Teutonic Order suffered a major defeat in the Battle of Tannenberg in 1410 at the hands of combined Lithuanian and Polish armies. At the end of Vytautas' rule in 1430, the expanse of Lithuanian-Polish territory stretched from near the Baltic to the Black Sea and the outskirts of Moscow to the border of Poland. However, Vytautas died shortly before he was to be granted the coveted title of King of Lithuania. Under the personal Polish-Lithuanian rulership, with the same person usually holding the title of King of Poland and Grand Duke of Lithuania, the loose union of Poland and Lithuania continued until 1569. The two lands were united under a commonwealth structure that preserved their dual sovereignty but placed the two states under a joint ruler and legislature. This partnership with Poland however relegated Lithuania to a subordinate role.

In the 16th century the Polish-Lithuanian kingdom faced a very formidable rival in the emerging Grand Duchy of Muscovy, when Ivan the Terrible, Russia's first Tsar, centralized his state and launched an expansionist drive. Poland declined as a territorial power when its lack of a strong monarchy made its political system less and less workable during the centuries that followed. It was perhaps not a surprise to many Europeans when at the end of the 18th century Poland-Lithuania simply disappeared from the map. Its three strong neighbors, Russia, Prussia, and Austria, carved up the entire kingdom in the three Polish Partitions of 1772, 1793, 1795, each claiming a part of the territorial Polish-Lithuanian spoils. Russia annexed most of Lithuania in 1795; a small section of western Lithuania went to Prussia and was named New East Prussia. This Prussian acquisition was of significance to my father's ancestors, for it was in that region that some of them, coming from East Prussia proper, presumably settled after it became a Prussian domain. A few years later Napoleon defeated Prussia in his wars of European conquest in 1807, and the French Emperor created the short-lived Duchy of Warsaw from the annexed Polish territories of Prussia and Austria. After the Alliance of Russia, Prussia, Austria, and Britain vanquished Napoleon in 1814-15, all of Lithuania, including the area that had been temporarily Prussian, was integrated into the Russian Empire.

Russian rule in Lithuania was moderate in the early years of the 19th century and granted considerable local autonomy to the native people. However, after Lithuanians participated in the Polish rebellions against Russia in 1830 and 1863, the Tsarist government intensified Russification. Russian law was imposed on the entire country and Lithuanian publications, normally using the Latin script, were outlawed. They could only be printed in the Cyrillic or Russian alphabet. The Catholic Church and Lithuanian schools were restricted. These unpopular policies stirred growing nationalist movements among the Lithuanian intelligentsia and also among segments of the early industrial workers in the towns and peasants in the countryside. Starting in the 1880s Lithuanian periodicals and publications were printed in East Prussia and secretly smuggled into Lithuania. They helped to raise the level of rural literacy and instilled nationalist attitudes. Nationalist political agitation toward the end of the century and during the first Russian Revolution of 1905 led to the formation of small political parties.

At the outbreak of World War I in 1914, the Lithuanian nationalist movement was submerged in the throes of the war but did not diminish. While under German military occupation and with the permission of the German imperial government, a conference of representatives of local governments and political groups convened a Lithuanian National Council in Vilnius in September 1917. It was this body that unilaterally proclaimed the independence of Lithuania in February 1918. However, this declaration could only be implemented after Germany's collapse in the war. A provisional government was established in November 1918 after the withdrawal of the German armies. It faced daunting challenges, for it not only had to create governmental institutions and administrative structures but

also provide for an immediate national defense against the incur-
sions from Bolshevik Russia and the newly restored Poland. Jozef
Pilsudski, the founder of the new Poland, embraced an ambitious
plan of resurrecting the medieval Polish-Lithuanian Commonwealth
and seized Vilnius and the surrounding region.

The novice Lithuanian government succeeded in creating the
Lithuanian National Army, which managed to drive the Red Army
out of Lithuania in 1920 but was unable to expel the Polish army
from the Lithuanian capital of Vilnius. Poland kept the city and surrounding region with its heavily Polish populace. As a result, fes-
tering hostility persisted between Lithuania and Poland until 1938
when the Warsaw government demanded that Lithuania reestablish
normal diplomatic relations with Poland or face war. Having no allies and being unprepared for war, the Lithuanian government had
no choice but to comply with the Polish ultimatum. In October 1939,
a few weeks after the defeat of Poland by the German armies, Stalin
pressured the Lithuanian government into accepting the stationing
of Soviet forces on Lithuanian soil. In turn, the Soviet dictator "re-
warded" Lithuania by restoring Vilnius and part of the surrounding
region to the now weakened Lithuanian state.

Trying to compensate for the loss of Vilnius and perhaps imitat-
ing the Polish example, Lithuanian forces occupied and annexed the
Memel (Lithuanian: Klaipeda) territory in early 1923, which had
been separated from Germany and placed under French administration by the Western Allies after Germany's defeat. This region had
a mixed population of Germans and Lithuanians, but had not been
part of Lithuania since the Teutonic Knights wrested it from Lithuanian tribes in the 1200s. The unauthorized seizure of the Baltic
port and land by Lithuanian military and paramilitary units soured
the relations between Lithuania and Germany during the years that
followed. However, the German government was in no position to
prevent the Lithuanian aggression, since the Allies had already sepa-

rated the region from Germany. In fact, fearing that Poland might gain control of it, the German government acquiesced in the merger of the Memelland with Lithuania, expecting it to be easier to reclaim it from Lithuania than from Poland at some future time. After Hitler came into power in Germany in 1933, the issue of the Memel region repeatedly caused friction between Germany and Lithuania. In March 1939 Hitler unilaterally compelled the Lithuanian government to return the Memel territory to Germany. The loss of the Vilnius area to Poland and the annexation of the Memel territory at Germany's expense - one forced upon Lithuania and the other self-induced - troubled its relations with its two most important neighbors when Lithuania was consolidating its state in the interwar period and needed foreign friends most.

On the domestic front, the constitution that Lithuania adopted in 1922 appeared to ensure that the country would follow Western models of parliamentary democracy. It provided for a strong unicameral parliament, popularly elected and based on proportional representation, which also included representatives of the ethnic and cultural minorities of the land. The president was chosen by the parliament and was accorded the right to appoint a prime minister. Catholic, socialist, and ethnic minority parties were beginning to develop functional roles in government. Nation building began however with a very small native leadership that lacked enough educated personnel to staff the positions of the state administration with competent personnel. Although numerous openings created career opportunities for Lithuanians and minorities, all too often semi-educated appointees and others politically favored but unsuitable for government service made for an inefficient and even corrupt administration (Vardys and Sedaitis 31).

At the same time, Lithuania faced formidable challenges in building its state and society during the twenty years of national independence. There were some notable achievements. Lithuania was able to standardize its language based on late 19th century reforms, which codified grammar and vocabulary, and established a fairly effective educational system. It also created some political and administrative institutions that energized national consciousness and provided the basis for statehood.

In national politics, the Lithuanian government pursued a rocky course that ended in authoritarianism. By 1926 corruption became the main electoral issue that toppled the Christian Democratic alliance, which had thus far formed the basis for a reasonably workable democratic government. Its collapse opened the door for a Populist-Socialist coalition. The new government, which could sustain itself only with the help of the small Polish and German minority parties, threatened the military and the Catholic Church with its proposals for reforms. Late in the year, nationalist army officers, overreacting to fears of communism and of too many cultural concessions granted to the Polish minority by the Lithuanian government, staged a coup d'état and overthrew the Populist-Socialist coalition government An authoritarian presidential government was established under Antanas Smetona with the rightist Augustinas Voldemaras as prime minister. Parliament was turned into a truncated representative body. Political parties were restricted or banned altogether except the rightist Nationalist party, which Smetona and Voldemaras had built up. Press censorship was enforced and limitations were imposed on private groups and organizations. Driven by extremist nationalism, the Smetona regime intensified the governmental policy of Lithuanizing employees of administrations, public and private enterprises, and educational institutions. Thus ethnic minorities found more and more of their rights curtailed and educational and gainful opportunities restricted. Smetona persisted in his conservative and authoritarian course until 1939. When he began to lose his grip, it was too late to save democracy and Lithuania's independence in the face of Hitler's and Stalin's imperialist aggressions into Eastern Europe.

Germans in Lithuania

One way to remind ethnic minorities that they owed loyalty to the Lithuanian state after Lithuania became independent in 1918 was through the government's insistence that all individuals who had foreign names must adopt a Lithuanized version. My German name Georg Blum became Jurgis Blumas in Lithuanian and accompanied me as long as my family and I lived in Lithuania before 1941. Among family and relatives I was known as Juri (pronounced Yuri), which could be taken to be Lithuanian or Russian. At the time I did not give any thought to names in general and my name in particular. But when my parents and I moved to Germany in 1941 and we immediately started using only our German names, I realized how odd it was that I had not been called by my given German names much before. Lithuanized names of my family, relatives, and German friends did not make me feel Lithuanian in any sense. In my early boyhood years I was aware that as an ethnic German I was somewhat different from most of the native people, since all my relatives, and I communicated with each other in German, a language not understood or spoken by the vast majority of the native populace.

In the late 1930s there were about 45,000 Germans living in Lithuania, which had a total population of close to 2.9 million. These ethnic Germans even at the high point of their presence constituted one of the smaller minorities in Lithuania compared to the largest minority of 200,000 Jews. The origins of Germans in Lithuania went back to the 13th and 14th centuries when individual German merchants moved to Lithuania. However, they rarely settled in large numbers and then only in cities like Kaunas and Vilnius. In the centuries that followed some German merchants and artisans spread into the countryside without establishing sizable colonies. Invasions coming from Tsarist Russia during the middle of the 17th century interfered with German settlements and forced most Germans in Lithuania to take temporary refuge in Prussia. More devastating in impact was the plague that struck certain regions of East Prussia and Lithuania in 1710; it almost wiped out the entire German population of Kaunas. The major German migrations into Lithuania came in the late 18th and in the 19th centuries; probably the largest number of Germans settled there between 1820 and 1830. Like my German Lithuanian ancestors these immigrants from East Prussia and some from the western parts of Germany came as farmers and artisans and established themselves primarily in the western regions of Lithuania.

My own paternal ancestors and many other Protestant families had originally migrated to East Prussia from the Salzburg region in Austria. In 1731 Archbishop Firmian, the ecclesiastical and secular overlord of the Salzburg region, attempted to enforce religious conformity in his domain by driving into emigration all of his Protestant subjects unwilling to convert to Catholicism. It is estimated that over 20,000 of these Salzburg religious refugees ended up in East Prussia, where the Calvinist Prussian king welcomed new settlers, since his subjects in the region had been badly decimated by the plague epidemic of 1709-11. Toward the end of the 1700s, my paternal ancestors migrated from East Prussia into Lithuania when, after the Third Polish Partition of 1795, a remnant of the dissolved Polish-Lithuanian kingdom was incorporated into the kingdom of Prussia as New East Prussia. The Prussian king needed farmers and artisans to populate this newly acquired territory, to develop its economic base, and to provide support for the military troops that he stationed there. Attracted by the opportunity to obtain farmland and greater freedom for artisans to become independent, Germans moved into the less populated regions of Lithuania in the late 18th and early 19th centuries and continued to do so for several decades even after 1815 when the area reverted to Russian rule.

German immigrants who came to Lithuania encountered not only a different language and culture but also different religious beliefs, for almost all Lithuanians were Catholics. The strict adherence to Evangelical Lutheranism gave Germans in Lithuania their distinctiveness and helped to preserve their identity in their chosen land into the 20th century. Once German settlers grew in numbers, they established their own churches and schools, providing institutional mechanisms that helped preserve cultural and linguistic unity among the otherwise often scattered families and groups. There were also a few German Baltic noblemen who came from the adjoining Courland during the 18th and 19th centuries and procured sizable estates, particularly in the northern part of Lithuania. A small number of other wealthy Germans came to own large farms, but the overwhelming majority of Germans in Lithuania were farmers with modest land holdings. Artisans, another major group of Germans, sometimes had to practice several trades and till some land as well to make a living.

Around the middle of the 19th century German workers and even some engineers moved to Lithuania to construct the first railroad that linked the German border town of Eydtkuhnen (after 1938 Eydtkau) to Saint Petersburg. Across the border of Eydtkuhnen, a bustling Lithuanian town named Kybartai developed with a significant colony of some 2000 Germans after WW I, and it held one of the most important German elementary and secondary schools in all of Lithuania until the beginning of WW II. Agrarian Lithuania was not suitable for the development of major industries, but a few German immigrants established breweries, leather works, iron works, and some other small factories. The largest German manufacturing plants were the metal and iron works founded by the Tillmanns family and the Schmidt brothers in Kaunas in the 1860s and 1870s. These plants employed 2500 to 3000 workers before World War I, half of whom were Germans. It was in the Tillmanns offices where my father found his early employment as a bookkeeper during the last years before the outbreak of the war in 1914. Germans living in

Kaunas in the early 1900s numbered about 4500, and Kaunas and the smaller Kybartai formed the largest German colonies in Lithuania until early 1941.

World War I brought many hardships for the ethic Germans in Lithuania. The Russian authorities looked upon them with great suspicion and forced a good many of them, especially from towns, to move to the interior of Russia. Thus my father, his brother, and one sister and their families were exiled to areas of western Russia. In 1915 German troops pushed the Russian armies eastward and occupied Lithuania. The German military administration extended certain advantages to the German minority of Lithuania and helped them to establish German elementary schools. Existing schools for Lithuanians were put under German supervision and were required to teach German. When Lithuania proclaimed its independence in 1918 and German troops withdrew after the war ended, most Germans who had been exiled to Russia returned to often plundered homes and impoverished living conditions. With the establishment of Lithuania as an independent state, Germans received Lithuanian passports and citizenship but, as mentioned earlier, also had to have their first and family names Lithuanized.

Thus a census conducted in 1923 undercounted the actual number of Germans living in Lithuania by many thousands. A corrected estimate placed the total of the German minority at 29,200, which was 1.4 % of the entire native population. In the 1930s the majority of Germans (about 58%) lived in the countryside and another 7% in villages and small towns. Townships larger than 2000 contained close to 35% of the German populace. It was estimated that 70% of Germans derived their livelihood from farming, since not only farmers but also artisans often owned some farmland. A fair number of impoverished Germans in the rural areas hired themselves out as farmhands and maids. German workers found employment in shops and factories primarily in Kaunas (Stossun 11-16).

Academically trained professionals among German Lithuanians were quite small in numbers. In 1939 one could find only three German lawyers, seven physicians, two dentists, and one veterinarian in all of Lithuania. Similarly, there were probably not many more than a dozen teachers and only nine pastors to serve thirty Lutheran congregations (Stossun 13). The few Baptist, Methodist, and other Free churches also had only a small number of trained pastors, and many of the congregations' needs had to be met by lay ministers. The lack of a large educated elite among the German minority explains why an effective leadership never emerged among them that might have allowed the German Lithuanians to play a more significant public role in Lithuanian society.

Methodism in Lithuania

Growing up as a German in Lithuania, I was a member of several minorities. In addition to the ethnic, cultural, and linguistic differences that distinguished me from the Lithuanians, my Methodist family background also singled me out among the Germans who were overwhelmingly Evangelical Lutheran. A few Germans living in Lithuania belonged to the Reformed faith of Calvinist origin and an even tinier group was Catholic. The Lutherans had found their way into Lithuania starting in the 16th century and came to include even some Lithuanians and most Latvians. (Both Latvia and Estonia are predominantly Lutheran to this day.) As more Germans immigrated into Lithuania in the 19th century, the number and size of Lutheran communities increased very substantially.

In the early 1900s some Free churches also sprang up among the Germans in Lithuania and developed a modest membership.

My family and my relatives in Lithuania were originally Lutheran, but a few became Methodists either before or after the First World War. The first Methodist congregation in Lithuania was organized in Kaunas in 1901 largely through contact with the German

Methodist Church in Königsberg (now Kaliningrad) in East Prussia. In 1905 a German Methodist pastor was appointed as the first regular minister in Kaunas and carried out missionary work in Lithuania and Russia. Before 1905 services had to be held in secret, since the Russian government did not grant freedom of assembly until the Russian Revolution in that year. The first Methodist church building in Lithuania was dedicated in Kaunas in 1911 and within a few years it was paid for with the help of the American Methodist Mission. Branch Methodist congregations were organized especially after the end of World War I in various towns in Lithuania, while Methodism also gained a significant foothold in Latvia and Estonia. Whereas most of the Methodist congregations in Lithuania were German, their counterparts in the other Baltic States were largely made up of Latvian and Estonian members.

In 1907 an American Methodist clergyman, Dr. George Simons, was appointed superintendent of the Finland and St. Petersburg Mission Conference. When the outcome of the war and the Russian Revolution that followed ended missionary activity in Russia and brought the political independence of the Baltic States, a new mission was organized and formally established as the Baltic and Slavic Mission Conference in 1924; it was superintended by Dr. Simons until 1928. All Methodist congregations in Estonia, Latvia, and Lithuania and their ministers were encompassed under this now largely American- sponsored church organization. The total number of Methodists in Lithuania probably never exceeded 1000 during the 1930s. They constituted a small fraction among the German Protestant group compared to more than 30,000 German Lutherans of Lithuania in the 1920s and more than 40,000 in the last decade before the outbreak of World War II.

References

Douglas, Paul F. *The Story of German Methodism: Biography of an Immigrant Soul.* New York, Cincinnati, Chicago: The Methodist Book Concern, 1939.

Eidintas, Alfonsas, and Vytautas Zalys, Alfred Erich Senn. *Lithuania in European Politics: The Years of the First Republic, 1918-1940.* Ed. Edvardas Tuskenis. New York: St. Martin's Press, 1997.

Heberle, Rudolf. *Die Deutschen in Litauen.* Stuttgart: Ausland und Heimat Verlags-Aktiengesellschaft, 1927.

Stossun, Harry. *Die Umsiedlungen der Deutschen aus Litauen während des Zweiten Weltkrieges.* Marburg/Lahn: J.G. Herder-Institut, 1993.

Vardys, V. Stanley, and Judith B. Sedaitis. *Lithuania: The Rebel Nation.* Boulder, CO: Westview Press, 1997.

Wagner, Gustav. *Die Deutschen in Litauen, ihre kulturellen and wirtschaftlichen Gemeinschaften.* Marburg/Lahn: J.G. Herder-Institut, 1959.

T W O

Growing Up in Lithuania

Ancestors

My family boasts neither of nobility nor high clergy among its ancestors. Both of my parents are descended from a lineage of humble farmers. My paternal family can be traced back with firm dates to my great-grandparents, Bernhard Blum (1815-1903) and Henriette Regge (1813-1899). They established the ancestral farm in Gulbinischken, a village about 32 kilometers (21.4 miles) east of what was once the German border. This community on the Šešupé River in historic Lithuania was then part of the Russian Empire. My great-grandparents' five sons and one daughter produced quite prolific offspring of their own. I don't recall hearing much about the life of my great-grandparents but more about the generation that followed. Their eldest son, Karl Blum, born in 1847 and died in 1927, was my paternal grandfather. Since he died before I was born, I never knew him except from sporadic mention in my father's family. After farming in an area not far from the ancestral seat, he acquired a farm that adjoined the family homestead in the 1870s. A skilled farmer, he also mastered the cooper's trade and mustered a fair amount of knowledge of laws and regulations, leading many a neighbor and friend to ask him for advice, or even to represent him in court. His first wife died early, leaving him with a very young daughter. He then married my eighteen-year-old paternal grandmother, Elisabeth Wiemer (1855-1944), who came from a village north of Kybartai on the German side of the border of East Prussia and Russia (after 1918 independent Lithuania). Her ancestors originated from the Salzburg region in Austria, from which many Protestants had been forced to emigrate in 1731-32 because they refused to convert to Roman Catholicism. Many of the Salzburgers found a new home and livelihood as farmers and artisans in East Prussia, where the Prussian King Frederick William I welcomed new settlers. My paternal grandfather also claimed Salzburg ancestry. Interestingly, the name Blum (in contrast to Wiemer) does not appear in church registers in the Salzburg region, but was found in East Prussian records as early as the late 1500s. My grandfather's Salzburg ancestors reportedly lived and farmed for several generations in the Suwalki area at some distance south of Kybartai, then part of Tsarist Russia.

Grandmother Blum or Oma, as German grandmothers are called, was a practical but gentle and generous person, whose winning personality was a legend among her grandchildren. I was too young to appreciate her story telling reminiscences of her parents and earlier generations but certainly felt her generous spirit in other ways during my visits to Gulbinischken. In old age she bravely endured the resettlement of the Germans from Lithuania in early 1941 and the family's return in the fall of 1942, with all the challenges of rebuilding a farm that had been neglected and lacked enough draft horses, cattle, and many of the necessary agricultural implements. On June 1, 1944, less than two years after her family returned to their home village, Oma died in her homeland and only six weeks before the advancing Soviet troops forced the German population to flee from Lithuania. From the union of my paternal grandparents came two sons, one of whom was my father, and five daughters; they all showed many of the admirable traits of their mother. More will be said about them later.

We have little information about the ancestral lineage of my mother's family and distant origins. Only a few birth-baptismal records and marriage certificates give clues about the approximate life span of my maternal great-grandparents and the region where they lived. I remember hearing very little about their actual lives, and I was remiss in asking my mother when she was still alive what she remembered about her grandparents and some of the relatives. My mother's immediate ancestors were born and lived in the Memel River region in East Prussia, not far from Tilsit. My mother's maternal grandmother, Aduzze Mikutaitike, was born in 1825, and married Salmons Tennikaitis, a farmer, in 1855. Another record indicates that my mother's paternal grandparents, Martin Poczka and Anna Maskolus, were united in marriage in 1863, and also farmed. It is interesting that the names of all of these maternal ancestors have a Lithuanian ring, suggesting that they were Germans who lived in a predominantly Lithuanian area of East Prussia and therefore used Lithuanized German names. It is possible that some were actually Lithuanian as by that time Protestants included many Lithuanians in that area of Prussia.

Both my mother and her parents were German citizens and culturally German, even though my grandfather's name on his baptismal certificate is indicated as Jons Poczka rather than the German Johann Potschka (1870-1940), which he seems to have used most if not all of his life. His wife Elsa Tennigkeit (1865-1944?), whom he married in Ragnit (near Tilsit) in 1897, is sometimes referred to as Tenikait. For a while my grandparents lived in the city of Memel (today Klaipeda) in the northern section of the Memel region (sometimes called Prussian Lithuania) before they became permanent residents of Tilsit in Germany proper. I never knew what kind of occupation my grandfather had. Later in his life he had become partially disabled and at times traveled and served as a lay preacher among Methodists and probably among some other Free Church followers during the 1920s and 1930s. My grandparents owned a two-story four-apartment building in Tilsit and derived much of their livelihood from the rents they received. But during the Great Inflation of Germany in the early 1920s, which destroyed the country's currency, they were forced to sell their property because rents were frozen and they could not keep up with taxes and maintenance expenses. Money became worthless in a matter of weeks during the hyperinflation and my grandparents were left penniless. They seem to have received some kind of small government support payment during the years that followed. My mother had no siblings and, I believe, only two cousins, one of whom I once briefly met. Her father reportedly had no siblings and her mother had only one sister that I remember being mentioned.

My own memories of my maternal grandparents are only of my grandmother, for I was too young to remember my grandfather's one time visit in Kybartai in the early 1930s. He died on one of his travels when hit by a train in 1940 and was buried unrecognized. My grandmother identified him when she was shown his clothes several weeks after the accident. When my mother and I stayed with Grandmother Potschka in Tilsit for several months during the war in 1942, she showed signs of dementia and was difficult to get along with. She could no longer write or see well and so it was difficult to keep in touch with her in the immediate years that followed. In the summer 1944 the retreating German front lines forced us to flee from German-occupied Lithuania to West Prussia and from that time on my mother could no longer get any reliable information from or about my grandmother. Thus my family never learned what became of her during the turmoil of the last stages of the war.

My father, Emil August Blum, was born in Gulbinischken in 1890, as the fourth child of my grandfather and his second wife. Even though of German descent and growing up in what was historic Lithuania, his citizenship was Russian as long as Lithuania remained part of the Russian Empire. He grew up on the family farm and often had to do agricultural chores when he would have preferred to do school work, as he remarked later. His early education was in a small elementary school in a nearby town, where the instruction by a teacher of German descent was in Russian except for religion and German, which were taught in German. He received further instruction from private tutors. For several years before World War I he worked in an office of a German-owned company in Kaunas and in various places of western Russia during a forced evacuation, due to his German ancestry, following the outbreak of the war in 1914. He was not able to return from Russia until 1921, where he experienced the turbulent Bolshevik Revolution of 1917 and the bitter Civil War that followed. In the meantime, Lithuania became an independent state and struggled to establish a new identity after centuries of foreign rule. After his return from Russia to his homeland, my father also faced a new challenge: rather than continue doing office work in bookkeeping and accounting, he felt called to the Methodist ministry. In preparation for it he entered the Methodist Theological Seminary in Frankfurt, Germany, in 1921, where he studied for three years.

In contrast to my father who grew up on a farm, my mother, Martha Maria Blum, née Potschka, knew farm life only from occasional visits of farms because she grew up in a city. She was born in Tilsit (now Sovetsk), East Prussia, in 1898. In her home city she attended German elementary and secondary schools and then a vocational business school. She also studied Lithuanian, which prepared her for secretarial work in Germany and Lithuania. In the mid-1920s my mother left her home city when she found work in Šiauliai, Lithuania, with a small Lithuanian company for which she handled primarily the German business correspondence. It was here where my father and mother met and were married in 1927.

To his regret, my father was recalled from seminary in 1924 before completing the usual four-year course, because the Baltic Methodist churches needed trained ministers badly. He served in several pastorates in Lithuania: Kaunas, Biržai, Šiauliai, Tauragé (the last three in north western Lithuania), and Kybartai. It was the custom of Methodist conferences in Europe and America to move their ministers every three or four years. It was in Kybartai where my father had his longest pastorate before assuming his last full time assignment in Lithuania in his home community Pilviškiai.

Kybartai is situated on the Lithuanian-East Prussian border in southwestern Lithuania and had a population of less than 7000 in the 1930s. It had a more cosmopolitan atmosphere than most other inland communities because of its proximity to Germany. The rather large German population had fairly ready access to the neighboring German border town of Eydtkuhnen (after 1938 Eydtkau). Some German families sent their children to secondary school in Eydtkau, after they had attended one of the German schools in Kybartai. Here my father served in a German-speaking Methodist church with a membership of more than 120, the second largest Methodist congregation in Lithuania after Kaunas.

My Early Years

I was born in 1932, making my entry a bit prematurely and not in a very robust condition. My Aunt Ottilie, the wife of my dad's only brother Karl, remarked right after my birth she hoped I would live long enough for my mother to recover from childbirth. There were comments later in my family that there had been a still birth or possibly two before my arrival. Sometime in 1933 or early 1934 I was joined by a younger brother named Alfred, who however died of pneumonia fourteen months later in 1935. I have few childhood recollections from my early years in Kybartai. I only came to know the town fairly well in the spring and summer of 1944 during the German occupation, when I was staying with a family friend while attending secondary school in Eydtkau. In contrast to the late twenties and thirties, there were no relatives of mine living in the community during the war, since none of them had returned to Kybartai after the resettlement of Germans from Lithuania to Germany in 1941.

In 1936 came a major change in my family's life: my father was assigned to assume the now full time Methodist pastorate of his home community Pilviškiai, a town situated in southwestern Lithuania. For at least two years prior to his transfer he had traveled regularly to Pilviškiai to preach and to perform some of the necessary church functions, including preparation of confirmation classes, while still serving as a full time pastor in Kybartai. One of my vivid childhood recollections of the time is when three horse-drawn wagons of my dad's relatives appeared to pick up all of our major belongings to move to Pilviškiai. On the way there they were surprised by heavy rain showers but our possessions survived in quite good shape, as far as I remember. My parents and I together with much hand luggage journeyed the twenty-mile route by train. Upon arrival at our new destination, we were not able to occupy our new home but had to stay for a while with my dad's sister and her family on the ancestral farm while my dad and several parishioners improved the wall insulation of the parsonage and made some badly needed repairs to make it inhabitable during the winter months.

Pilviškiai in the 1930s had a population of less than 3000. During Lithuania's independence in the prewar period it served as a township seat. The surrounding region of the town was almost exclusively agricultural, but within the township there were some industrial and commercial enterprises, including a fur-processing plant, several mills, an oil press, several small factories, and dairy and farm equipment repair shops. The population of the town was fairly diverse. The vast majority of the inhabitants were Lithuanians, but there was also a significant presence of Germans and Jews. Our family physician and dentist were a Jewish couple with whom my parents generally conversed in German. So were several of the shopkeepers in the community, whose Yiddish I could understand before I learned some Lithuanian. I do not recall encountering any Russians or Poles except as occasional visitors. Even though the community lacked the more interesting cultural atmosphere of Kybartai, for my father it was a return after a good many years to his home region where two of his sisters with their families, including his mother, and numerous cousins lived.

The surviving copy of a thank you letter that my father wrote in November 1936 to an unnamed pastor of an American Methodist Church for a contribution toward retiring some of the Pilviškiai congregation's debt gives an impression of the Methodist congregation that he had taken over. It had only fifty-one members, most of whom were farmers and artisans. Twelve years before, the small congregation had bought a lot on which the church members together with the minister had built a modest church hall and an adjoining parsonage. The congregation had to borrow funds to finance the original construction of the church and parsonage building. The economic difficulties of the 1930s, caused by the Great Depression and exacerbated by an agricultural trade war with Germany in the middle of the decade, hit farmers especially hard. Many church members suffered reduced incomes and thus found it very difficult to sustain the local congregation and also to pay off the church debt. For the years before 1936 the Pilviškiai congregation had to make do without a regular resident pastor and depend on the assistance of ministers from other churches. Most of the Methodist churches in Lithuania were still dependent on the support of the American Church Mission, which was never able to meet all the needs of the slowly expanding church communities.

Even though I was not much aware of the tight financial circumstances of my parents, I did notice that there were some things that my family went without. There was no running water in the house or an indoor toilet. We had electricity unlike most families on farms but no radio or fancier furniture that I occasionally saw in more affluent homes. In the summer of 1938 my father took a second job as an assistant bookkeeper in Kaunas in order to supplement the family income. This meant he had to get up very early in the morning every weekday to catch a train for Kaunas at the local train station, which was almost two miles from our home. He would return in the early evening on ordinary workdays and by early afternoon on Saturdays. In addition, he had to prepare Sunday sermons in German and sometimes also in Lithuanian as well as Sunday school lessons and teach a confirmation class in the spring. From time to time there were baptisms, weddings, and funerals, all of which required special attention. My mother was also engaged in the church as accompanist on the harmonium during services and as choir director. There was a small but quite active brass choir, which fortunately did not require the minister's attention, since a member of the congregation directed it. Such a heavy engagement could not help but take its eventual toll. As a result, my father was planning to leave the full time ministry once he found a better paying outside job, presumably also in Kaunas. In a letter that my Aunt Olga Reinert, dad's youngest sister, wrote in January 1939 to Aunt Emilie Fischer and her husband Adam in Minneapolis, she attributed my dad's plans to my "clever" mother. In family affairs my mother was inclined to take more initiative than my dad. She was the one who had to make everyday food and household purchases, and was thus keenly aware that a preacher's compensation was too meager to sustain a family indefinitely. Starting in early 1941, the decision to withdraw temporarily from the ministry was made for my dad when we resettled in Germany and it was not feasible for him to continue in the ministry during the war and its immediate aftermath until 1946.

My boyhood memories of the years in Pilviškiai are quite happy ones. As an only child I learned to occupy myself but always welcomed playing with other children. Until I entered elementary school in 1939, my association was with German-speaking cousins and second cousins and, occasionally, other children who came to Sunday school. It was always a bit of a treat when my parents visited Aunt Olga's farm, next to the original homestead of my dad's family, usually on Sunday afternoons, or on festival days like Easter

Monday, Whit-Monday, and at Christmas time. We would be picked up usually by one of my cousins in a horse-drawn carriage during much of the year and in a sleigh if there was enough snow in the winter. I especially enjoyed spending time with my cousins on the farm to play; and then there were edible treats from our grandmother. At home my parents taught me how to read and write in German and before long I could read simple fairy tales on my own rather than have one of my parents or one of my teenage cousins relate or read them to me. Apart from the usual Christian church festival days, there were not many special occasions observed in my father's church.

However in May 1937, Bishop Raymond J. Wade and his wife paid a day's visit to Pilviškiai. His visit fell on a weekday but every effort was made to observe the occasion with as much congregational participation as was possible on a normal workday. Two photographs that were taken at that time give a glimpse of the event. Most people turned out in their Sunday best; the church brass choir performed; there was a dinner for the guests, and some members of the congregation, for which my mother and her sister-in-law, Aunt Olga Reinert, had prepared days in advance. Since the Bishop and his wife spoke only English, everything had to be translated. Bishop Wade, who came from Indiana, was assigned to the Scandinavian, Baltic, East European, and West European areas as the presiding bishop of the Methodist Church in the late 1920s and continued to serve until 1939, when the beginning of World War II disrupted the direct link between continental European and American Methodism. I became personally acquainted with Bishop Wade after the war when he visited Stuttgart in 1948 and my father and I made a special trip to meet with him. In 1956, on the occasion of the meeting of the Methodist General Conference in Minneapolis, he and his wife came to my parents' home in Minneapolis while I was a senior at Hamline University. From thereon we exchanged regular Christmas greetings until a few years before he died in 1970. Bishop Wade was somewhat formal and conservative in his demeanor but also engaging with younger people.

A regular celebration on a grander scale, considering the attendance of many relatives from out-of-town, was held every year on the family farm in Gulbinischken at the end of June, on Peter and Paul Day, a holiday. It was always a big family reunion but also included some members of Methodist churches, especially from Pilviškiai, Kybartai, and Kaunas. Combined brass choirs performed and my father usually gave a short devotion or sermon. This event was especially enjoyable for the older youths, who swam in the nearby Šešup⊠ River and did much socializing. The older relatives spent their time getting reacquainted, leaving us youngest ones to fend for ourselves with childhood games that had us running all over the farm yard and in the nearby fields. Other childhood memories bring back for me the occasional visits together with my parents or one of them to Kaunas. Sometimes I would be left there to stay with Aunt Alma Schulz for a week. Her son Alfons was five years older than I, so I did not have that much in common with him. My main entertainer was my Uncle Karl Blum, who in his retirement had extra time on his hands, and happily took me on pleasant short excursions to visit the local airport, some museums, or other nearby relatives. Among the edible delectables that my Aunt Alma served was a rare banana. I never remembered what it was called then until years after the war when I came to eat some regularly in the United States and was reminded of its taste.

1939

My fairly peaceful, free childhood came to a sudden end in 1939. The first reality that struck me was the requirement to attend elementary school once I turned seven. According to Lithuanian law, mandatory schooling began at age seven rather than six as was common in many other countries. When I started elementary school in the spring of 1939, it came as quite a shock to me to enter a school environment in which I hardly understood a word. There were no German schools in the community where we lived and my parents were not prepared to send me to a German school in Kybartai, for that would have required putting me in a boarding school. I was already able to read and write in German. Now it was simply a matter of learning to do the same in Lithuanian. Both of my parents were fully fluent in Lithuanian but used it only in my presence when they did not want me to understand what they were discussing. My school teacher did not speak any German. I usually tried to do the best I could without always understanding her instructions. I could also fairly easily imitate what my Lithuanian classmates were doing on their exercises and on the homework we were assigned. In addition, my mother kept in touch with the teacher and helped me develop a Lithuanian vocabulary at home, in part by using some New Testament passages, since some of these were familiar to me in German. Naturally there was a lot of rote learning but children tend to learn quite quickly some of the basics. Beyond time in school, my parents enlarged my circle of friends by introducing me to several Lithuanian children in the neighborhood and inviting them to come and play in our backyard.

This at first painful Lithuanian schooling experience lasted a little over a year and was interrupted by the fairly long summer vacations that were customary in Lithuania. During these vacations we were assigned to work on writing of words and short sentences by filling several notebooks. It was largely rote work. In less than a year I felt quite at home in the use of the Lithuanian language, since I had acquired a fairly good child's vocabulary and did not seem to have any particular difficulty communicating both in speaking and writing. When facing the challenge of schooling in what seemed to be an unfamiliar company, I accepted the inevitable as something that I could not change. It was a good introduction to foreign language study in my later years. Once I switched to German schools after our temporary resettlement to Germany and during our short-lived return to Lithuania under German occupation, I felt no desire to keep up my child's command of Lithuanian and, as a result, what I had learned fairly quickly but did not regularly use was also gradually forgotten.

The Lithuanian school that I attended was less than a mile from my home and I almost always walked there by myself. That was my first childhood experience of going somewhere on my own without being accompanied by one of my parents or an adult. It gave me an early sense of independence. After I turned eight, my parents allowed me, on several occasions, to take the three mile hike to the family farm in Gulbinischken for short visits on my own. There was little danger of my getting lost in town or in the countryside as long as I kept taking the familiar routes. The only time things became a bit more complicated was in the fall of 1940 when a small epidemic of the hoof and mouth disease struck some cattle in the community and the town authorities put the community in quarantine. The main streets had check points where all people entering and leaving had to disinfect their footwear by dipping their soles in a basin of disinfectant. On one or two occasions the street that we lived on was temporarily blocked for all foot traffic, and I was not allowed to take my usual way home from school. That was an occasion when I had to figure out on my own how to find a detour through an unfamiliar part of the town to reach my home.

Adjustment in school was my main preoccupation in 1939, but in the late summer and fall of that year the second reality that began to make my and my family's life less predictable was the darkening cloud of national and international crises in Europe. They were triggered by Adolf Hitler's aggressive expansionist moves, which culminated in the violent eruption of World War II in Europe in

September. My parents and I had some control over my schooling, although the options were limited. But our personal future became uncertain when the governments and hapless peoples of the Baltic States found themselves victimized by the designs of Nazi Germany and Soviet Russia.

At the time, I was not yet accustomed to following domestic let alone international news. But I could not help but pick up comments of adults about political and international events that appeared to be of increasing concern to them. Naturally I had no idea what impact, if any, these happenings might have on the life of my family, the German minority, or the life of Lithuanians. All I sensed as a young boy was that my parents and their occasional conversation partners expressed some anxiety about the future of the country and us as members of the German minority.

Lithuania found its peace and its very existence increasingly threatened by the actions of its neighbors Poland, Germany, and, after September 1939, the Soviet Union. The very unfriendly relations with Poland after it had seized the Vilnius region from Lithuania in 1920 came to a head when the Polish government demanded in 1938 that Lithuania establish diplomatic relations with Poland and accept the cession of Vilnius as a fait accompli, or face war. The second blow to Lithuania's pride and territorial integrity came in March of the following year when Hitler forced the Lithuanian government to return the Memel region to Germany, which the Lithuanians had grabbed in the aftermath of World War I. The unilateral German expansion into Lithuania was merely the follow-up of Nazi moves after the annexation of Austria and the Sudeten region, the rim of Czechoslovakia in 1938, and the dismemberment of the remainder of that hapless state in March 1939. Now it was only a matter of months before Hitler invaded Poland and unleashed World War II.

In the wrenching developments leading to the outbreak of the war, Lithuania had no friends among the European powers. In the face of diplomatic concessions to Poland and the territorial loss to Germany, Lithuania suffered injured pride as well as territorial loss, but did retain her tenuous political independence. She tried to steer a neutral course in the emerging conflict of the major powers. But that was not enough to save Lithuania's independence when Hitler and Stalin concluded a cynical agreement in late August 1939, which brought another partition of independent Poland and the Baltic States. Between 1772 and 1795 the famous historic Three Partitions of Poland-Lithuania perpetrated by Russia, Prussia, and Austria had wiped this medieval state off the map. Now Nazi Germany and Soviet Russia repeated history by carrying out the fourth partition of this region. It enabled Hitler to embark on his planned aggression against Poland and bought Stalin some time and a better defense line before he was to become embroiled in the conflict of the major European powers. The published text of the 1939 Nazi-Soviet Pact said nothing of a territorial division of Eastern Europe. Its specific terms were contained in a secret protocol of the pact that did not become known until after the end of the war when the Western Allies captured German diplomatic documents. I myself learned of these terms when I wrote a term paper as a junior in college in the mid-1950s on the Nazi-Soviet Pact and read the published documents that included the secret clause. The Soviets in fact officially denied the existence of such a secret agreement until 1991, almost the very end of the Gorbachev era. In 1939 we heard only rumors of the specific provisions of the territorial changes that divided much of Eastern Europe between the two totalitarian powers.

My parents did not own a radio but they had the use of one for a limited time in the summer 1939, and I still remember hearing the news of the German invasion of Poland and parts of Hitler's Reichstag speech on September 1. The British and French war declarations followed shortly after the German attack against Poland, launching World War II in Europe. People in Lithuania were anxiously wondering what was coming next and how the rapid German conquest of Poland would affect Lithuania. Quite early there was a rumor among the Germans that we would not have to be too concerned since Lithuania would fall under German domination. As I learned from my work on the college history term paper, the secret protocol of the Nazi-Soviet Pact at the end of August did indeed state that much of Poland and all of Lithuania would be part of the German sphere of influence, whereas the rest of Poland, Estonia, and Latvia would be claimed by the Soviets. However, the boundaries of the division of the territorial spoils between Hitler and Stalin were changed significantly at the end of September 1939, again by secret protocol, after the Polish armies had been totally destroyed by the superior German forces. Soviet troops in turn had occupied, without having to fight, a large section of eastern Poland starting September 17. Stalin was intent on adding all of Lithuania to the other two Baltic States as his domain, for it had once belonged to the Tsarist Empire and strengthened his eastern defense lines. Since Germany wanted to continue receiving raw materials from Soviet Russia, Hitler was willing to trade Lithuania for Lublin and the Polish provinces around Warsaw. However, Germany insisted on keeping a strip of southwestern Lithuanian territory which adjoined the Suwalki region and comprised districts around Mariampolé. According to a map in the documents, the Šešupé River that flows through the western section of Pilviškiai formed part of the eastern boundary of the contested Lithuanian border strip. Had the German claims prevailed, my parents' home would have remained under Soviet domination, whereas Gulbinischken, less than three miles west, where our immediate relatives lived, would have been incorporated into the German domain. Since Stalin did not formally abandon the contested area from his claim to all of Lithuania and even "accidentally" occupied it with the rest of Lithuania in July 1940, disputes persisted over the final settlement into January 1941. An agreement was reached with Ger-

many when the Soviets paid 7 ½ million gold dollars, the price that
the U.S. had paid for Alaska in 1867, as compensation for keeping
this Lithuanian section and also German property claims in Estonia
and Latvia. The rumor that Germans would not have to move from
Lithuania lost credibility fairly early, but with the uncertainty about
the future of the Lithuanian border strip at least some Germans residing in that area of Lithuania might have had reason to believe it.

A short time after the Nazi-Soviet Pact had been signed and the
German invasion of Poland had begun, Berlin proposed to the Lithuanian government to enter the war against its long-standing foe Poland and to seize the Vilnius region. The Lithuanian President Smetona and his government rejected the offer, insisting that Lithuania
wanted to realize its national aspirations only by peaceful means.
When however in October 1939 Stalin offered a mutual assistance
treaty to the Lithuanian government with the proviso that 20,000
troops would be stationed on Lithuanian soil, Smetona and his ministers were helpless to refuse it. The Soviet dictator sweetened the
bitter pill of Soviet military intervention by returning the historic
capital Vilnius and a reduced section of the surrounding region to
Lithuania.

In the early months of Soviet military presence in Lithuania, the
life of the native people was not much affected, since the occupying
troops, who outnumbered the Lithuanian national army, were kept
in bases and there was little interference by them in the everyday
affairs of the country. Stalin was too occupied trying to subdue the
stubborn Finns during the winter months of 1939-40 to extend his
full sway over Lithuania and the other Baltic States. The established
Lithuanian government continued to function fairly normally and
the living conditions of the populace did not seem to change very
noticeably. Food was still quite plentiful and most other goods continued to be available in shops and stores as in earlier years. There
did not appear to be any particular constraints on free movement.

The local Lithuanian officials, policemen, and post office workers were left in their positions and carried on their work, as did the private businesses, small factories, and shops of Pilviškiai and other communities. Some scarcities became noticeable in early 1940 when sugar was not always available in the food stores and some items of manufactured goods became more expensive or temporarily disappeared from the stores. The real worsening of conditions came with the expansion of Soviet control over the political, economic, and social life of the country starting in the summer of 1940. It marked the beginning of the Sovietization of Lithuania.

1940: Lithuania Becomes a Soviet Socialist Republic

After the Russo-Finnish War ended with Finland's submission to Stalin in March 1940, the Soviet dictator decided to take full possession of all Baltic lands. The rapid defeat of France by Hitler's armies in May and June gave him the convenient moment to strike against the Baltic States, leading to the overthrow of the Baltic governments and total occupation of their territories. Lithuania was his first victim. After several weeks of severe diplomatic pressure, Kaunas was handed a midnight ultimatum on June 14 to replace its government with compliant ministers that would carry out Soviet directives, while the Red Army began to pour masses of troops into Lithuanian areas. President Smetona, with the support of a few of his ministers, advocated symbolic resistance, but was outvoted in a critical cabinet meeting. Fearing arrest and deportation to the Soviet Union, he and several of his officials hurriedly fled the capital and crossed the border into Germany. A contemporary cartoon that I remember well had Smetona wading with rolled-up pants through the shallow stream that separated Lithuania and Germany. He did not stay in Germany but found his way to the United States, where he died in 1944.

Before the summer of 1940 I only heard of Russian soldiers

from what my father reported about observing Soviet military units marching through the streets of Kaunas, where he worked during the week. When large numbers of Soviet troops and a growing contingent of political personnel streamed into Lithuania after the mid-June ultimatum, the strain on foodstuffs and the shortage of goods in stores was felt almost immediately. The large purchases of Red Army and Soviet civilian personnel could not keep up with the production of goods, the stock of which had declined even before the military occupation. Also, the distribution of goods was disturbed by the presence of the foreign forces, which resorted to requisition when normal purchases were not readily available. Store owners and many people began to hoard whatever scarce goods remained. My parents and I did not experience any outright shortage of the most necessary foodstuffs (in contrast to consumer goods), for we could still buy bread, potatoes, some vegetables, even butter and meat at the market or in food stores of Pilviškiai, although only at higher prices. In addition, we could get help from Aunt Olga Reinert's farm, my grandfather's homestead. Novelties that my father remembered from his years of exile in Russia during World War I were the watermelons of southern Russia. They appeared in large quantities in Lithuanian markets and in food stores, but were received with little enthusiasm by the local populace. A more painful and disturbing Soviet import was the Russian ruble that by the end of 1940 replaced the Lithuanian currency, the *litas*. The exchange rate was very unfavorable for Lithuanians, for 0.9 ruble was declared to be worth 1 *litas,* whereas the normal exchange rate had been 3 to 5 rubles for the same amount of Lithuanian currency. Many of the Soviet military and political personnel, who commanded high ruble incomes, garnered windfall returns and further depleted the declining supply of goods.

In October 1940 my father gave up his job as bookkeeper in Kaunas. I don't remember hearing any comment as to the reason.

It may have been that the firm that he worked for was facing expropriation, as happened to many companies and larger businesses after the summer of 1940. However, it was more likely my father decided to leave his job, expecting changes for ethnic Germans in Lithuania after the resettlement of the German minorities from Estonia and Latvia to Germany in 1939 and early 1940. I also do not remember whether losing the additional income worsened my parents' difficult financial condition. When my maternal grandfather died after being hit by a train in the spring of 1940 and my mother made a special trip to Tilsit to see her mother, she possibly brought back a modest amount of German hard currency from my grandmother, which would have helped. In any event, they had some money even to extend a loan of several hundred rubles to Aunt Olga when she asked for it late in 1940.

After the full Soviet occupation began, some of the most ominous changes in the normality of Lithuanian life were political and these were soon felt in the country. Even though a coalition cabinet headed the first Lithuanian government, as instituted by Soviet demand, it comprised only Soviet nominated Lithuanian ministers and officials including several communists in key cabinet positions. They had no choice but to carry out Moscow's constitutional and political directives. These provided for a transitional "People's Government" that held a national election in mid-July to form a People's Assembly. The results of the election were manipulated and falsified, for despite a low popular participation, as later testimony and documents outside of the communist sphere confirmed, they proclaimed that 95.51% of eligible voters had participated and of these 99.19% had voted for a union list of communist and nonparty candidates. When the elected candidates met on July 21 as the new People's Assembly, they quickly proclaimed the establishment of a Soviet Socialist Government and by resolution asked the Supreme Soviet in Moscow to admit the Soviet Socialist Republic of Lithuania into the Union of

Soviet Socialist Republics. The Supreme Soviet formally "granted" the request on August 3, 1940 (Vardys and Sedaitis 50-52; Misiunas and Taagepera 28-29).

Though the average Lithuanian was perhaps not overly aware of the political manipulations at the higher governmental level that were delivering all inhabitants of the land into the hands of the new foreign regime, no one could help noticing the changes that were rather quickly occurring even in smaller communities. Dismissals of higher administrative, police, and even school officials became common. Often lesser known individuals, some of whom professed to have been "Communists" for years, replaced them. My parents and I were surprised to hear that one of the plumbers in Pilviškiai, whom we personally knew, was now openly professing his communist persuasion of long duration.

Surveillance in public was becoming common and many people watched themselves in what they said loudly in public and who seemed to be observing or following them. My parents firmly admonished me quite early that I was never to tell anyone outside our home what they or others had discussed inside our walls. I believe they also kept some of the more sensitive information from my ears to begin with. My parents' only typewriter which was used for church and private correspondence had to be registered with the authorities. The police required my father to submit multiple sheets with a sample line of every individual letter and some full words produced by the keys of the typewriter. On election days individuals that we generally did not recognize would come to the door to remind my parents to go and vote. The reaction among Germans was however that they would try to stay away from election polls.

One concession that my parents made to escape harassment, first from Lithuanian nationalist zealots and now communist enthusiasts, was to fly the prescribed flag on flag days. During the years of Lithuanian independence our house displayed the national Lithuanian flag, marked by yellow, green, and red stripes. After the establishment of the Soviet Socialist Republic, the national Lithuanian colors were forbidden and replaced by the red hammer and sickle banner. Many flags at that time were hastily cut and sown from red material that was more commonly used for pillowcases or covers of featherbeds; the hammer and sickle emblem was usually painted or pasted on these flags. My mother found some rather attractive red color material and made a flag from it but without the hammer and sickle. No one seems to have noticed the omission of this essential communist symbol when the flag was flying from our house. Flags were not the only means that the authorities used to drum the heroic image of the communist regime into public consciousness. I remember the very large pictures of Stalin, sometimes together with Lenin, which were prominently displayed on the front walls of some public buildings in town. Smaller portraits of contemporary Soviet leaders like Vyacheslav Molotov, Mikhail Kalinin, and Marshal Kliment Voroshilov, in addition to the historic icons of Marxism-Leninism-Stalinism, Karl Marx and Friedrich Engels, frequently adorned the windows of office buildings and some stores to familiarize the populace with the new ruling elite and their forebears. They took the place of Lithuanian political and historical figures, whose image was being carefully eradicated from display if not the consciousness of the Lithuanian people.

The appearance of new public officials, the propaganda in the newspapers, the barrage of images of strange names, and the occasional appearance of Soviet soldiers even in towns like Pilviškiai, all created an atmosphere of insecurity and apprehension. What heightened fears of the average citizen were incidents of violence that we did not just hear about but actually observed. Before the advent of the communist regime damage done to farm properties by arsonists was rare. But in 1940 such incidents in our region increased dramatically. It was especially German farmers and mill owners whose barns, stables, or mills suddenly went up in flames, generally only at night. It became a dreaded sight to watch the sky illuminated by large red fire balls and to know that the property of someone we very likely knew was burning to the ground. Generally the arsonists escaped unknown and one could only speculate if these acts of destruction were perpetrated to intimidate only certain families or were actually directed against the German community. Fortunately, the farms of all our immediate relatives escaped this kind of wanton destruction.

The most unnerving fear that began to spread among many members of the communities was the prospect of arbitrary arrest by the authorities, which in many cases also meant eventual deportation to the Soviet Union. Reports about the feared knock during the night or early morning hours were spreading quickly. I don't recall hearing about arrests of specific persons in Pilviškiai during the time when we lived there under the new regime, though I suspect there must have been some. In the first year of Soviet occupation about 12,000 persons were arrested in Lithuania for alleged political and economic "crimes." In mid-June 1941, the Soviets rounded up an estimated 34,000 Lithuanian men, women, and children and loaded them into freight cars for deportation to the "inland" of the Soviet Union (Vardys and Sedaitis 54). Until the removal of all ethnic Germans to Germany in early 1941 (related in the next chapter), German families seemed to have had some protection against arrest as a result of the Nazi-Soviet agreement. Nevertheless, several hundred Germans in Lithuania were imprisoned, including my Uncle Oscar Schulz, Aunt Alma's husband, who lived in Kaunas. As a small businessman he apparently fit one of the arrest categories. In November 1940, a Soviet document, later captured after the German invasion, listed 14 categories of individuals among the Lithuanian population scheduled for deportation. It included, in addition to politicians, military officers, higher civil servants, gendarmes, industrialists, businessmen, estate owners, political émigrés, foreigners, also clergymen and all individuals with personal foreign ties (Misiunas and Taagepera 41). If we had not been able to leave Lithuania in winter 1941, my father would have been at risk of being arrested and deported. According to the list, he qualified in two categories: he was a pastor who served under an American bishop and had ties to Germany and the United States.

References

Blum, Arkadius, ed. *Unsere Familiengeschichte eingebettet in die Geschichte unseres Volkes und der Weltpolitik von 1731 - 1981.* Augsburg: J. Walch, 1983.

Lachauer, Ulla. *Paradiesstrasse: Lebenserinnerungen der ostpreussischen Bäuerin Lena Grigoleit.* Reinbeck bei Hamburg: Rowohlt Verlag, 1996.

Misiunas, Romuald J., and Rein Taagepera. *The Baltic States: Years of Dependence 1940-1990.* Expanded and updated edition. Berkeley and Los Angeles: University of California Press, 1993.

Sontag, Raymond James, and James Stuart Beddie, eds. *Nazi-Soviet Relations, 1939-1941: Documents from the Archives of the German Foreign Office.* Westport, Ct: Greenwood Press, 1976. Reprint of 1948 edition published by the U.S. State Department.

Vardys, V. Stanley, and Judith B. Sedaitis. *Lithuania: The Rebel Nation.* Boulder, CO.: Westview Press. 1997.

THREE

Resettlement

Removal to Germany

The conclusion of the Nazi-Soviet Pact in late August 1939 came as a shock to many in Europe and the world. It defined territorial interests of the two totalitarian powers in Eastern Europe, which effectively divided the region between them, and gave Hitler a free hand to attack Poland. Another stark surprise to the Germans living in the Baltic States and the Eastern European countries was the Nazi-Soviet agreement made at the end of September 1939, after the Polish campaign ended. It changed some of the boundaries in the partition of territories between Nazi Germany and Soviet Russia they had agreed upon in August and especially stipulated that Reich nationals and persons of German descent residing in territories under Soviet domination would be allowed to move to Germany. In turn Germany was to permit persons of Ukrainian or White Russian descent in territories under German control to migrate to areas under Soviet rule. Though the actual text of the agreement remained secret, the planning for its implementation was not kept from the public. German people had been living in the Baltic States for six or even seven hundred years. Most of the ancestors of the Germans in Lithuania had settled there in the 1700s and 1800s so their descendants represented the third or fourth generation of German families. They regarded Lithuania as their homeland, though they retained their German cultural identity and much of the German language. Now with little warning and by a mere stroke of the pen, such Germans in Eastern Europe and the Baltic region were urged to leave their centuries old ancestral homes and move to Germany.

It is now known that plans for a resettlement of ethnic Germans

from Eastern Europe to Germany had been under discussion in the
upper echelons of the SS, the elite political paramilitary Nazi organization, as early as 1936. The considerations for a removal of sizable German groups from foreign countries touched on the economic and social problems that Germans suffered in the lands they lived
in and anticipated shortages of labor within Germany. In October
1939 Hitler made his rationale for a resettlement of Germans from
Eastern Europe known in a Reichstag speech. He pointed to the need
to remove some of the causes of conflict that were generated by minorities in states. He asserted it was utopian to assume that "a high
quality people" like the Germans could be readily assimilated by the
countries they lived in during a time when the principle of nationality and race was paramount (Stossun 28). One of the real motiva-
tions for the removal of Germans from Eastern Europe advocated
by the SS leadership became clear after the resettlement had been
completed in early 1941: Heinrich Himmler, the Reich leader of the
SS, now proceeded to recruit many young ethnic German men for
the Waffen SS, the military arm of the Nazi elite organization.

Hitler's speech on the removal of ethnic Germans from Eastern
Europe caused much sensation and encouraged those Germans of
Estonia and Latvia who were fearful of living under Soviet occupation. At first, Germans in Lithuania did not show undue concern that
they feared for their future, even after the resettlement of Estonian
and Latvian Germans began in October 1939. But many became ap-
prehensive after Soviet domination of Lithuania turned oppressive
and was followed by full occupation of the entire country.

In the Nazi-Soviet negotiations in late September, Joachim von
Ribbentrop, the German foreign minister, reached an agreement
quite early with Vyacheslav Molotov, his Soviet counterpart, on the
idea of a population transfer (Stossun 27-28). However, the implementation of the actual removal was subject to separate treaties. The
preparations for the resettlement of the ethnic Germans were left

to their organizations in the respective countries. In 1939 and 1940 the transfer of Estonian and Latvian Germans and German minorities from Soviet-occupied eastern Poland and the Soviet annexed section of Rumania was carried out and completed. The Lithuanian Germans had to wait.

In Lithuania it was the Kulturverband der Deutschen Litauens or Cultural League of the Germans in Lithuania that served as the principal agent for dissemination of information among the German minority. It also assembled the personnel that helped register all Lithuanian Germans and made a statistical survey of their assets and property after early reports of a resettlement were spread in the fall of 1939. The Kulturverband had been formed in the 1920s to promote German schools and to sustain German cultural awareness among the ethnic Germans in Lithuania. After the mid-1930s, it increasingly advanced political ideas and also tried to promote the economic concerns of the Lithuanian Germans. The Lithuanian authorities were intent on limiting the rights and influence of minorities and therefore looked with suspicion upon many of the activities of the Kulturverband. They kept it under close surveillance much of the time and also interfered with its endeavors. After the Soviets occupied all of Lithuania in 1940, all political, economic, social and cultural organizations were forbidden. However, the Kulturverband was allowed to continue its activities and the publication of the German newspaper *Deutsche Nachrichten für Litauen* (German News for Lithuania). The membership of the organization had fluctuated between 1000 and 3000 before the fall of 1939, but increased dramatically to 10,000 by early 1940. The German embassy in Kaunas, which the Soviets also allowed to remain open, ensured significant protection of the Lithuanian Germans before their resettlement. The embassy also used the Kulturverband to provide reliable information for the Germans of Lithuania and to carry out the organizational tasks in preparation for a successful resettlement.

Before 1939 my parents were aware of the activities of the Kulturverband but did not have any ties to it. They tried to maintain neutrality vis-à-vis an organization that had a narrow German focus in the pursuit of its programmatic objectives. As citizens of Lithuania, they felt that keeping out of political involvement, whether Lithuanian or patriotic German, was a safer way of maintaining religious autonomy and ensuring relative freedom for church work. This must have been even more urgent in the later 1930s when the Kulturverband began to adopt some Nationalist Socialist slogans and helped organize youth activities among Lithuanian Germans that had close ties to Nazi Germany. There is no evidence that anti-Semitism played a significant role in the programmatic and organizational efforts of the organization despite what was happening in Hitler Germany.

My parents had no doubt that they would leave Lithuania for Germany if a resettlement became an option. My father had experienced the First World War in Russia and had lived through the turmoil of the Bolshevik Revolution and Civil War, and thus had a stark recollection of early Soviet Communism in practice. He did not want to live under a communist regime again. My mother, who had grown up in Germany, knew the German order (though not the Nazi order), and could readily compare it to what she was now experiencing in the deteriorating conditions of Lithuania, was most adamant that we must leave Lithuania when there was a chance.

The onset of the war did not at first bring any noticeable changes in the life of my father's congregation or the role of the Methodist church in Lithuania. Before the total occupation of the country by the Soviets, church activities pretty much continued as they had for years with services on Sundays, including Sunday school, some prayer meetings during the week, and choir practices. In 1939 even the annual evangelization week was held, but this time without a visiting pastor from a Methodist church in Germany, as had been customary during many of the preceding years. With the Sovietization of Lithuania after June 1940, the political atmosphere in the country ominously worsened and put churches on notice that they too would be affected in their religious autonomy.

The occupying Soviet authorities, working through their communist Lithuanian appointees, attempted to provide central direction but could or would not control the arbitrariness of local level authorities. An attitude of lawlessness and caprice marked the behavior of the new local administrative officials in their treatment of the community citizens. Such conditions left room for unpredictable interference in citizens' lives by officials of the local administration and police without people knowing what was permissible and what was punishable, let alone where to appeal for redress. No one seemed accountable for the actions of authorities. When the usual church festival days like Easter and Christmas were eliminated as recognized holidays, my father's congregation continued to observe them and so did the local German Lutheran Church and the Lithuanian Catholic Church. As far as I know there were no immediate repercussions from that, but no one could predict what authorities might do in the future.

Both my parents and our immediate relatives carried on with daily life as best as we could under the worsening political and economic conditions, but also began to plan for resettlement to Germany after the early summer of 1940. It meant keeping tuned to whatever news could be obtained from the *Deutsche Nachrichten* of the Kulturverband or informally by word of mouth from German friends and acquaintances about developments that would make emigration possible. My parents subscribed to the *Deutsche Nachrichten für Litauen* in 1940 to follow closely what the Kulturverband offered by way of suggestions and directives in preparation for a resettlement. Still, they felt no need to become actual members of the Kulturverband.

The volunteers of the Kulturverband who began the registration of Lithuanian Germans and their property in the late fall of 1939 continued throughout much of 1940. After the autumn of 1940, the Kulturverband concentrated exclusively on resettlement activities and became in practice the auxiliary arm of the cultural section of the German foreign office, operating through the German embassy in Kaunas. As the Sovietization drive intensified, Lithuanians, including Lithuanian Germans, were arrested in significant numbers and their property frequently expropriated. Thus the Lithuanian German community felt growing urgency to see resettlement get underway. There was relief when it was announced in September 1940 that negotiations had begun between the German and Soviet foreign offices to formulate a treaty. After some lengthy deliberations a formal treaty was concluded in January 1941, stipulating in detail the terms under which the resettlement of Lithuanian Germans was to be carried out. In addition, the treaty provided for the transfer of Lithuanians, Russians, and White Russians from the Memel region and Suwalki area to the Lithuanian Socialist Republic.

My father quit his job in Kaunas in October 1940, so he no longer needed to commute from Pilviškiai to the city that had only one year before lost its distinction of being the capital of Lithuania. However, most important governmental functions continued to be centered in Kaunas, especially the German embassy, rather than in the newly reestablished historic capital Vilnius. My mother was relieved not to see my dad travel every weekday when life was becoming more difficult. And as resettlement loomed closer at hand, there was much work to do to get ready for the removal, while continuing with many of the church activities. Christmas and the New Year were observed as in the past but the old spirit that marked the celebration of these festival days was fading in the face of the oppressive communist regime and anxiety about the future of those of us who hoped to leave.

Toward the end of January 1941, several weeks after the resettlement treaty had been signed, the German Resettlement Commando appeared in Kaunas to begin implementing the removal plan for the population transfer. The German delegation was divided into teams that covered the 15 districts of Lithuania. A parallel Soviet organization, consisting of NKVD (Secret Service) officers, worked with the German representatives in organizing the actual removal of the Lithuanian Germans. Time pressure was acute, since the full removal of the German minority was to be completed by March 18. The harsh winter weather with snowstorms and frequent subzero temperatures made the work of the German Commando and the resettlers so much harder. Some members of the Commando had to travel many miles by sleigh or even on foot to reach the ethnic German farmers in the most remote areas of the country. The largest burden of the work fell on those who would soon leave their homes or farms. They had to dispose of some property and possessions, prepare for trekking if they were farmers, and pack the limited amount of household goods and furniture they were allowed to take with them (Stossun 33-52, 75-91).

In January and February my father crated the furniture, including our harmonium, and packed large wooden boxes or chests with books and a few household goods, all of which in aggregate could not exceed 25 cubic yards. Our most valuable piece of furniture sent to Germany, an oak wardrobe, we never saw again. It reportedly was destroyed in a bombing raid. We suspected it was stolen, since near Danzig (Gdansk today) where it was temporarily stored, bombing raids were still rare before late 1942. My parents were so busy attending to all the details for the removal to Germany, including documents, settlement of various personal affairs, and packing that they completely forgot about my ninth birthday until a week or so later. This was the only time it ever happened. My parents' mood during those frantic days and weeks was however upbeat. They were elated and looked forward to the transfer to Germany as a welcome relief in the face of a dreaded future under the Soviet communist regime.

Until the very last day my parents were harassed by one particular local Lithuanian communist official. He repeatedly came to our house to check on what my parents were packing, whether they were taking along items that were supposed to remain with the house, etc. As his last aggravation the day before our departure, he wanted to confiscate all the keys of the padlocks of our outdoor storage places after locking them. My father had planned to use these locks to secure several of the trunks that we were having shipped. This particular trouble maker harassed others too and must have acquired quite a reputation as the local horrid hellion of the new regime. We heard he was among the first to be shot after the German invasion of Soviet Russia started in June 1941.

Our exodus came toward the end of February. The day before our departure one of my cousins came and took some of our belongings that we had to leave behind including my dog Karo, who now returned to the family farm where he was a puppy. For me that was a sad day but dogs were not allowed to be taken to Germany. We would not have done so even if that had been an option, but Karo had been my loyal companion and a playmate. My parents and I were lucky to stay together as a family during our resettlement to Germany. The families of our immediate relatives from the farms had to travel separately, because males over fourteen had to remain with the horse-drawn wagons and cattle during the transport to the German border, where they were put on a freight train for transfer to East or West Prussia. It took months before the men were reunited with their families. Some of the elderly like my grandmother were also moved separately and temporarily sent to locales other than their families' designated camps in the German Reich.

Women and children of the farmer families joined those of us who remained together as families. We were all put on a passenger train in Pilviškiai and transferred to a German train in Eydtkau, our closest border crossing in Germany. For Germans coming from other parts of Lithuania, two additional German border towns served as transfer points. At the Lithuanian-German border Russian guards were exceedingly strict in searching whatever baggage was taken into Germany. Passengers traveling by train could carry only limited hand baggage: 100 pounds for the head of the household, and half that amount for the other adults. Frequently the Russian border guards even confiscated items allowed under the treaty terms. For instance, women were permitted to take with them one fur coat and usually also a valuable fox fur, but the guards often liberated them of the latter. My mother had a self-made animal fur (not a fox fur) which she was permitted to keep only after much hassle. Other favorite items for confiscation included silk stockings and some jewelry. Farmers were allowed to take two horses, one cow, three hogs, and ten hens, as well as some smoked ham, bacon, and a pail of lard. It was the latter that enterprising border guards frequently confiscated, who amassed large collections of lard pail "trophies" at border crossing points.

When the resettlement was completed in March 1941, a little over 50,000 Lithuanian Germans had been removed to Germany under quite humane conditions with special consideration given to the elderly and the ill. The German Resettlement Commando in Kaunas had however some difficulty getting all of the arrested ethnic Germans released. I remember my cousin Arkadius, who was a member of the German Commando, reporting that my Uncle Oscar Schultz was only released in the end when the head of the Commando insisted his group would not leave until he was freed for transfer.

All German resettlers, both young and old, went voluntarily, though with varying degrees of enthusiasm to Germany, a land that most really did not know. Many of the younger generation fancied the resettlement to Germany as an opportunity to continue life under new and better conditions with more employment opportunities.

Most older people and especially farmers had mixed emotions about leaving homes or farms that often had belonged to their families for generations. Nevertheless, most recognized that remaining in their homeland under the Soviets was not a prudent option. During the same time that ethnic Germans were leaving Lithuania, about 20,000 Lithuanians, White Russians, and Russians were moved, at times by force, from the Memel region and the Suwalki area to Soviet Lithuania.

Arrival in Germany

The transports of German resettlers from Lithuania were given a friendly reception at the German border. The Eydtkau railroad station was decked with bunting and a low level Reich official uttered some words of 'Welcome home to the German Reich.' And there were flags. The new flag that we had to become accustomed to was the swastika banner, which looked benign to us compared to the repulsive red hammer and sickle colors of the Soviet Union that we left behind. It was only later that we learned of the swastika's sinister meaning. As for our destination, I don't think my parents knew where the German train was to take us. At station stops on the way into the interior of eastern Germany, we were treated to sandwiches, coffee, and other refreshments. The less than twelve-hour journey ended in Stargard, a small town about 35 miles south of the well known city of Danzig (now Gdansk) in West Prussia. Here at a camp, we shared a large room with bunk beds with some forty other people, right next to a mental institution.

As a toddler with my dad's hat and cane, 1933.

My parents and I when I was three, 1935.

Part of my father's congregation in Pilviškiai when Bishop Wade visited in 1937. Second row seated: my Uncle Karl Blum, Mrs. and Bishop Wade; I am between my parents.

When I was twelve, 1944.

I am fourteen, 1946.

Class picture of the sixth grade of the Backnang Oberschule after our comprehensives in 1950 with two of our teachers. I am in the back row, fourth from left.

My Aunt Olga Reinert with her sons Emil, between my parents, and Albin,
on her left, came to say goodbye to us in Schwäbisch Hall in January 1952.

My Aunt Emilie Fischer with my parents in the backyard of her
home in Minneapolis, 1955.

The German authorities in charge of the resettlement program had taken over military barracks, hotels, facilities of churches, and other accommodations to provide temporary housing for the flow of ethnic Germans from Lithuania in different locales of East and West Prussia and some former Polish areas. The ethnic Germans from Estonia, Latvia, and Eastern Europe, who had arrived earlier, had usually been resettled in private housing that was found for them in the former Polish areas of West Prussia and the recently annexed sections of western Poland. Polish inhabitants had been forced out of their homes in these regions and pushed into the interior of the German-occupied Poland. By the time the Lithuanian Germans arrived, there were not many such private accommodations left. This shortage necessitated the concentration of the newcomers in camps. Despite German planning, quite a few of these reception centers turned out to be inadequate and became a source of early disillusionment for many resettlers, especially from Lithuania, who had come with high expectations. We were lucky to be placed in one of the supposedly "better" camps.

For those unfortunate families whose wives with young children were separated from their husbands and older sons, it often required frustrating weeks just to establish contact with each other and then months before such families were reunited. As I recall, my parents heard from our immediate relatives quite quickly, even though it took many months or even a year before we managed to visit them in camps or at their new permanent location. Both my parents did volunteer office work for the camp administration and thus became acquainted with several of the uniformed SS officials in charge. Such a contact made our stay somewhat more personal and my parents also met several native civilian Germans, who helped to familiarize us fairly quickly with the town of Stargard and even the large city of Danzig. Within a few months my father started some kind of office job with a private company in the nearby town. Also after two or three months of barrack style living quarters, we were assigned a room that we shared with only two other single strangers. We all had to take our meals in a large dining hall and had to get used to rationed portions, which sometimes had been further diluted by dishonest kitchen staff, who reportedly lived and ate better than the rest of us. Fortunately from time to time we could still buy smoked fish, some potatoes, even some pastries in stores in town without ration cards. However, many of these food items were expensive, and my parents had limited funds. I remember both my father and I always welcomed fried potatoes that my mother prepared in our room on an electric hot plate from time to time to supplement our daily community fare.

There were fairly regular classes for school age children and all in German at last. However, the instruction was not very systematic and sometimes the elementary school was more like kindergarten. Here I learned for the first time about the "heroic" life of Adolf Hitler and the dynamic history of the Nazi movement. The camp administration also scheduled movies from time to time. For children there were fairy tale films like *Snow White and the Seven Dwarves* or *Sleeping Beauty*. Adult movies often had a strong anti-British propaganda overtone; they dealt with historic subjects like *Ohm Krueger*, the leader of the Boers in South Africa, who resisted the British, or *One Life for Ireland*, the story of an Irish resister who lost his life fighting the British in World War I. After all, Germany was at war with Britain.

Toward the end of May, a "flying commission" appeared in our camp to conduct the processing of all camp inmates and to carry out naturalization proceedings. It consisted of officials and staff drawn from the *Einwanderungszentralstelle* or Central Immigration Authority that had been established to screen ethnic German resettlers to determine whether they met the criteria for naturalization and integration into the German Reich. We all had to undergo a fairly comprehensive physical examination in addition to an evaluation of our family and cultural backgrounds, which were checked for German ethnic and racial lineage. The outcome of this screening decided where families would be allowed to settle. Those who were recognized as "fully" German were granted immediate German citizenship and were qualified to live in eastern Germany and annexed areas as well as German-occupied territories in Eastern Europe. Generally, mixed marriage families, where one marital partner was Lithuanian, Polish, Russian, or families who were not fully German in cultural heritage, were excluded from settling in the newly annexed German areas in the East, i.e. the territory recently taken from Poland. They were also barred from Lithuania to which some 20,000 resettlers returned during the German occupation in 1942-43. People who were not regarded as pure Germans were permitted to live only in central and western Germany. The intention was to enable them to become more quickly assimilated into the German populace, i.e. more "Germanized." Such families were not necessarily deprived of eventual German citizenship but definitely restricted in the choice of their future residence. This constraint was harsh on farmers who thereby lost all chance to acquire a homestead of their own either in the Germanized sections of Poland, where Polish families had been forced from their land, or later in their homeland. They had to settle for work on farms of others or accept alternate employment. Quite a few non-farming Lithuanian Germans were assigned work in war related industry. Young men were generally drafted into the German army or the Waffen SS, the party related military formation. Interestingly, the Waffen SS consisted of half non-German units toward the end of the war.

My parents and I passed the naturalization screening without difficulty and were granted German citizenship. My mother had become a Lithuanian citizen when she married my father in 1927, and apparently no special note was taken of her original German citizen-

ship for she and I were simply included on my father's naturalization certificate. Even after becoming German citizens we were not
always free to go on visits as we wished. The camp was periodically
quarantined and all outside travel was forbidden. This was true in
June 1941, for instance, and most likely was due to the pending major military action in the east.

On the morning of June 22 came the stunning news that the German armed forces had begun the invasion of Soviet Russia. We now
know that Stalin was shocked, even though he had received numerous
warning signals of Hitler's impending attack. Lithuanian Germans
followed with intense interest the rapidly advancing German front
lines which crossed Lithuania in a matter of days, not weeks. I remember watching freight trains carrying guns and military vehicles
to the front lines from a highway overpass not far from our camp. It
was exciting to see the Soviet "enemy" retreating so quickly. Only
later did we learn that two of my cousins, Arkadius Blum and Eugen
Pluskat, were among the German front line troops that moved into
the Russian spaces. Arkadius survived the war but did not return to
Germany until 1954, having endured 9 1/2 years as Soviet prisoner
of war. Eugen Pluskat was among the early ones killed in action.

Life for us in the camp did not change much in the immediate
months after the German attack on the Soviet Union. My father continued to work outside the camp and my mother kept her part time
job in the office of the camp administration. My father observed
with concern that more and more of the Polish employees in the
offices of the company where he was employed were losing their
jobs and were being replaced by German employees. This experience prompted him to reject any prospect of settling in former Polish territories.

After the naturalization processing was completed in the fall of
1941, many German resettlers from Lithuania were shifted around.
Those who had been designated to live only within the borders of

pre-war Germany (as of 1937) were gradually transferred either to camps or selected regions of the interior of the German Reich. My parents and I were moved to a camp in Soldau in south East Prussia in late October or early November 1941. Here we shared a fairly large room with two or three families. The advantage of the new location for us was that we were rather close to the camp where my father's sisters, Aunt Olga Reinert and Aunt Wanda Blum with most of their families, had ended up and we were able to visit each other. I continued in whatever school there was in the new camp until two weeks before Christmas when I developed the mumps and was whisked to a children's hospital. It took my parents a little while before they found out where I had been taken. This was the first time I had been separated from my family and sent to unfamiliar surroundings. My recovery proceeded normally and I was very happy to be released after ten days, just in time not to miss out on whatever Christmas observations were offered for children in the camp. Traditional religious services or ceremonies were not permitted in the camp but Santa Claus did come to present gifts to children and we had the usual richly decorated Christmas tree. Since the German words "Weihnachtsbaum" for Christmas tree and "Weihnachtsfest" for Christmas do not suggest a narrowly Christian reference, as they do in English, the Nazis did not have to invent new names for whatever was related to Christmas but only eliminate Christian religious content

My father was under the jurisdiction of the German Resettlement authority and so had little choice but to accept whatever positions he was given for employment. Thus a return to the Methodist ministry even in Germany, where churches continued without much interference of the Nazi government, was not an option. In German-occupied Lithuania no German churches were permitted to reopen. My father was fortunate that he had certain business skills, which qualified him for different office type assignments. He remained exempt from military service throughout the war due to a childhood illness, which had left him with a shorter right leg. The same impediment had also kept him out of the Russian army in World War I. In early February 1942, my father was assigned a job as a bookkeeper in a meat products company in Königsberg (today Kaliningrad), the capital of East Prussia.

Finding work in the German war time economy was generally not difficult, especially since much of it was by assignment. It was much more difficult to find housing. During the time my father was employed in Königsberg, a city of several hundred thousand inhabitants, he found only a room to rent without cooking facility and had to take his major meals in the company cafeteria. Both of my parents hoped that something might be found where my mother and I could join him. They spent several weeks in the city looking for some accommodation, while my mother and I were camping out in a hotel.

While we were briefly staying in Königsberg, the historic city of the Prussian kingdom where the king was traditionally crowned (not in Berlin!), my mother and I had a chance to visit the castle, the major historic museum, the cathedral, and some other well known sights of the city. I found the museum especially fascinating. All of these memorable historic places were either damaged or destroyed during the war or in the aftermath. When the Soviets annexed the northern half of East Prussia in 1945, they rebuild Königsberg with typically Soviet structures, effacing pretty much its 700 years of Prussian history. Only the ruin of the cathedral was partially restored after the war, but full restoration did not get underway until the 1990s, after the collapse of the Soviet empire. While on a tour of the Baltic States and Poland in 2002 with my son Alfred, we observed that this sole surviving major monument of Prussian and German times still needed a good deal more interior repair. Whatever remained of the castle after the destruction of the war was blown up in the late 1960s. Close to the castle's old site the Soviet government began to construct a rather massive H-shaped House of Soviets, a city hall, in the early 1970s. This monstrous Soviet architectural erection was never completed for its foundations turned out to be insecure. It continues to stand as an ugly reminder of the notorious mismanagement of the Soviet Communist regime.

Other happy encounters in Königsberg in 1942 were several visits with Arkadius, my cousin, who had been granted a leave from his service on the eastern front to continue his university studies in economics and foreign languages. He managed to write a doctoral dissertation but was not able to get it processed, and thus was never awarded the doctoral degree.

When no other accommodations could be located in Königsberg, my parents decided that my mother and I would move in with my grandmother in Tilsit, my mother's hometown, instead of returning to the camp in Soldau. Tilsit, today known as Sovetsk, is located in the northern section of the former East Prussia and right on the Memel (Neman) River. During the war it had a population of about 60,000 inhabitants. Historically, the city is best known for the Peace of Tilsit of 1807, consisting of treaties between Russia and France and Prussia and France. Napoleon, who had defeated Prussia in battle, exacted a very high territorial price from the Prussian king, forcing him to accept the breakup of his kingdom. Some of the negotiations between the French Emperor and the Russian Czar Alexander had taken place on a raft in the middle of the Memel River, while the Prussian royal loser paced the shore. A small historical museum in town, which I repeatedly visited, commemorated this humiliating event in pictures and some artifacts. In the end, the alliance of Austria, Prussia, Russia, and England defeated Napoleon and thus the very punitive provisions of the Peace of Tilsit did not stand. The city of Tilsit was quite badly destroyed during the end phase of World War II. Today under Russian rule very little of its Prussian and German historic past remains, even architecturally, except the Queen Louise Bridge, named after the wife of the Prussian king, who unsuccessfully pleaded for clemency in 1807 with the victorious Napoleon.

For my mother, the return to her hometown after more than a decade and a half of absence brought mixed experiences. She still had some friends in the city and numerous acquaintances, who sometimes helped with advice and support. But my grandmother's mental state was not very good. Old age was beginning to cloud her mind and perception of others, which made it difficult to maintain a harmonious relationship with her. She lived in an upstairs unit of the four apartment complex that she and my grandfather had been forced to sell during the Great Inflation of the early 1920s. It was the only apartment that did not have electricity in the building and probably in that section of the city. After dark the available lighting came from smelly kerosene lamps. I never heard a good explanation of why my grandparents did not have electricity installed when it came into use. The apartment did have a gas stove and thus did not lack some modernity.

Soon after we had moved to Tilsit, I was enrolled in a nearby elementary school. It was my first experience with an established German school that had some tradition and continuity. I did not have any difficulty keeping up in school in any of the subjects. What I missed was having regular friends, since I was new to the school and the neighborhood where we stayed did not have many children of my age. In part I compensated for it by immersing myself in some of the history books in my grandmother's home, including books my mother had used when she was a schoolgirl. Since these books were of pre-Nazi vintage, they had the attitude and tone of the German Empire before World War I, which gave me a different slant on Prussian and German history than I was getting in school. It was patriotic and a bit anti-British and somewhat more anti-French, but it did not carry the condemnation of foreign influence and the castigation of the post-WW I Treaty of Versailles that was characteristic of Nazi history texts. Since I had visited several of the historic sites in Königsberg, especially the castle and the museum that illustrated so much of the Prussian past, reading about some of the leading personalities among crowned rulers, ministers, and generals became so much more meaningful.

However, school was not all that was now to be part of my life. I had turned ten and therefore was obligated to join the Hitler Youth. For girls there was the comparable League of German Maidens. These two organizations encompassed ten-to-eighteen-year-old German boys and girls and were divided into two formations: the Jungvolk or Young People for ten-to-fourteen-year-old boys, Jung-mädel or Young Maidens for ten-to-fourteen-year-old girls, and the actual Hitler Youth and League of German Maidens for the fourteen-to-eighteen-year-olds. Membership in these organizations had become compulsory in 1939 for all German youths. By tagging along with one of my classmates, who was already a member, I joined a musical Jungvolk troop. We had regular meetings every Saturday afternoon and frequently also one or two meetings during the week after school. To an outsider many of the activities might have appeared to be those of a glorified military youth troop. We had fairly regular drills and marching, some gymnastics and sports, and occasionally military type games. We also had to learn several Nazi songs and were orally quizzed on how well we knew the important events of Hitler's life and the history of the Nazi movement. There were anti-Semitic overtones in some of the presentations and emphasis on the purity of the Aryan race and how it was different from other (inferior) races. Beyond that indoctrination was fairly moderate at least during the time I belonged to this particular troop. We also had to collect scrap metal and lime blossoms to make a practical contribution to the war effort. Discipline was strictly enforced, especially attendance at meetings and the obligatory collection events.

When I once skipped a Saturday afternoon meeting because my dad had come to visit for the weekend, I was mightily chewed out at the subsequent meeting for neglect of duty.

Later in the fall I was transferred from the musical unit to a regular Jungvolk troop together with my schoolmate who had led me to this group, since neither one of us played an instrument and thus we were considered unfit to remain in this specialized youth formation. I found this new association more congenial because the leader of the troop that I was transferred to happened to be the son of one of my mother's friends, who took some personal interest in me to ease the transition. By that time of the year, we also had more indoor events than in the summer and early fall. One that I remember especially was a commemorative observance of the Langemarck episode in the World War I Battle of Ypres (Belgium) in October and November 1914, in which half-trained German military units consisting of high school and university students were mowed down in large numbers by well entrenched British machine gun fire. The idealistic young soldiers reportedly marched into the Allied firing lines singing "Deutschland, Deutschland über alles," expecting to obtain through patriotic zeal what fire power prevented them from achieving. Though German nationalists and National Socialists celebrated this event as a mark of the heroic spirit of sacrifice for the German Fatherland, more sober historical judgment called it the *Kindermord of Ypres* or Massacre of the Innocents at Ypres.

During her late teens and young adulthood in the twenties my mother had belonged to the Baptist Church of Tilsit. Services were still being held during the war and my mother and I attended several of them. How careful pastors and laymen who occupied the pulpit on Sunday mornings had to be was driven home to us when one of the laymen in a sermon remarked that the German people will have to answer for what was being done to others by some Germans. Within a week this man was arrested and taken to a concentration camp. Obviously a spy in the audience had reported him to the Gestapo, the Nazi secret police. He was not released until many weeks later and then reportedly only because his son, an officer in an elite military unit, had intervened on behalf of his father.

One of the sad memories that has remained with me from my time in Tilsit is seeing several times two German Jewish children with their mother on a street nearby my grandmother's house. They all looked forlorn and showed signs of poor nourishment. From September 1, 1941, Jews living in Germany were required to wear a yellow Jewish Star on their clothes in public and were thus easily identified. For several years they had been barred from public transportation and public events, were forced into restricted housing units, and could purchase their much reduced food rations only during limited shopping hours. Jewish children could not attend German schools. I do not know how many Jews remained in Tilsit in 1942, since they were being moved in large numbers from German cities to ghettoes in Poland and increasingly to the death camps. One day my mother observed the former Jewish owner of the leading Tilsit department store looking into the show window of the store that he had once owned. A week later she heard from a friend that he had committed suicide with a note saying, "Germany was also my fatherland." These terse last words epitomize the great tragedy of German Jewry brought on by the Hitler regime. Most German Jews had been integrated into German society, identified with German culture and German history, and at times were even more patriotic Germans than many Germans. Quite a few of the Jewish families had joined the Lutheran Church and embraced Christianity. Many thousands of Jewish men served in World War I as soldiers and officers and gave their lives for the country that they considered to be their fatherland. But during the war years of the Nazi regime even German Jewish men who had earned high decorations and promotions during the Great War ended up being shot or gassed for no reason except that they belonged to a "race" that the twisted Nazi mind declared to be inferior and a mortal enemy of the superior Aryan race. At this stage in the war, I was aware that Jews were being removed from Germany to the "east" but learned only one or two years later that many of them were also being murdered.

References

Loeber, Dietrich A., ed. *Diktierte Option: Die Umsiedlung der Deutsch-Balten aus Estland and Lettland 1939-1941.* 2nd unchanged edition. Neumünster: Karl Wachholtz Verlag, 1974.

Stossun, Harry. *Die Umsiedlungen der Deutschen aus Litauen während des Zweiten Weltkrieges.* Marburg/Lahn: J.G. Herder Institut, 1993.

F O U R

A Short Sojourn before a Long Flight

A New Beginning

Integrating the resettled Germans from Eastern Europe into the enlarged German Reich proved challenging for the German authorities. Except for those resettlers who were deemed not to be fully "German" to Germanize the newly annexed lands, the Germans from Estonia, Latvia, Bulgaria, Bessarabia, eastern Poland, and Yugoslavia were assigned to live in the re-annexed West Prussia and territories taken from defeated Poland. A few German resettlers from Lithuania, including my Uncle Karl Blum and Aunt Alma Schulz and their families, all from Kaunas, were also among them. Early resettled Germans were often given furniture, household goods, and dwellings that had been seized from Poles and Jews who had only recently been removed. But the great majority of the Lithuanian Germans were the last to be resettled, and living in crowded camps, they became increasingly disillusioned and disheartened. There were few places left in West Prussia and the annexed former Polish territories to absorb more newcomers. As a result, several months after the start of the German invasion of the Soviet Union in June 1941, Nazi authorities began to make plans for returning most of the Lithuanian Germans from the camps to German-occupied Lithuania.

Another reason was that the civilian German occupiers of Lithuania feared that many of the former German farms would become unproductive and wasted unless more enterprising and reliable cultivators were put in charge. After the Germans had left their farms in Lithuania in the late winter of 1941, the Soviet authorities frequently assigned the empty German homesteads to Russians coming from the interior of the Soviet Union and Lithuanian families, who had been removed from the Memelland and formerly Polish regions. Many Lithuanian German farmers eventually returned to their former homeland either to take over their old homesteads or to take charge of farms that had previously belonged to Jewish, Polish, Russian, and some Lithuanian owners. Generally, Lithuanian owners of farms before the Soviet occupation were allowed to remain on their homesteads.

The previous resettlement of the Baltic Germans from 1939 to 1941 was to save them from the Soviets; the return of the Lithuanian Germans to their homeland in 1942 and early 1943 was intended to advance the Nazi plan of Germanization of large areas of Eastern Europe. It is notable, however, that the German resettlers from Lithuania who returned to their homeland did so voluntarily if not enthusiastically, expecting to resume their livelihood in familiar surroundings.

A first group of Lithuanian German farmers from the camps were sent to Lithuania in March 1942. Their task was to prepare for the return of the many Lithuanian Germans that followed later in the summer and the fall. Aunt Wanda's husband Karl Blum (my other Uncle Karl), who farmed the original family homestead in Gulbinischken before 1941, was sent back in July and assigned to his old farmstead. His family and Aunt Olga Reinert with her two youngest sons, Gustel and Olgart, and Grandmother Blum followed in October. Aunt Olga and her sons also reclaimed their family's farm. Their Lithuanian neighbors, as did many Lithuanians in the countryside, welcomed the returning Germans with open arms. To them the return of the Lithuanian Germans appeared to promise the restoration of stable conditions in the country and gave them some assurance that they would not have to fear another Soviet occupation, which had brought so many hardships and large deportations of Lithuanians to the Soviet Union.

My relatives who came back to their old farmsteads endured

daunting challenges and hardships for many months. In many ways they had to start all over again. The horses and the livestock that they had taken to Germany during the resettlement in the winter of 1941 had been distributed among East Prussian farms and were gone. It was fortunate that Uncle Karl's and Aunt Olga's farms were close together so that the two families could help each other. At first they had to make do with whatever few animals were left on the farm; with time they were able to acquire additional ones from neighbors and the German authorities, who later brought some horses and cattle from East Prussia. The buildings of Aunt Olga's farm had all survived the start of the German invasion of the Soviet Union in June 1941. However, practically all of the furniture in the farmhouse was gone. Uncle Karl's and Aunt Wanda's family was much less fortunate. The only building that was left on their farm was the badly damaged house, but the barn, stable, and cowshed had burned down during the fighting. With great difficulty Uncle Karl managed to rebuild these structures from the materials that could be salvaged from deserted farms in the vicinity. He had little outside help except from his seventeen year old nephew Gustel, Aunt Olga's son, who took time away from his mother's farm to help out. His two older brothers, Emil and Albin, had been drafted by the German armed forces and were able to visit only on short leaves. Gustel himself was also later to be drafted in the summer of 1944 after his family was evacuated from Lithuania. He did not return from the war, but died presumably in action in the early months of 1945.

By the summer of 1943 most of the reconstruction had been accomplished and the Blum and Reinert families were now able to concentrate on farming. I enjoyed several pleasant visits to Gulbinischken in 1943 while my parents and I were living in Vilkaviškis, which was half way between Pilviškiai and Kybartai. As an eleven and twelve-year-old I still remembered quite vividly the green meadows, well cultivated fields, and the Šešupé River of Gulbinischken from my earlier boyhood days. This time I took these short weekend visits on my own. My last visit was together with my parents in early June 1944 on the occasion of my grandmother's funeral, which also turned out to be the last family reunion in Lithuania. I remember thinking how different some houses looked both on the outside and the inside after being away less than two years from the farms and nearby Pilviškiai where I had lived. The familiar buildings and rooms appeared to be so much smaller than I had remembered them.

In October 1942 my father was recalled from Königsberg by the German Resettlement authority for assignment in Lithuania. He was given the task of opening a food ration card office for all Germans in the county of Vilkaviškis. This was a fairly large county, and had had the highest concentration of Germans before 1941 in all of Lithuania. My mother and I followed my dad in late November from Tilsit. In the first few months after our return our housing consisted of two small rooms on the second floor of the same building where my dad had established his office, on the ground floor along with several other German offices.

In the early weeks and months, my dad had no support staff to operate the ration card office. People often came from long distances and then had to stand in line for many hours before they could leave with their ration cards in hand. My mother and I helped in the office as best as we could in order to expedite the issuing of the ration cards. On one occasion my dad had a health collapse due to overwork but fortunately recovered fairly quickly. Since school had not yet opened for German children in Vilkaviškis at that time, I did not mind working long hours in my dad's office. Quite a few weeks later, after strong appeals from both of my parents to visiting German officials from the German civilian government center in Kaunas, my dad was given funds to hire the necessary secretarial staff and the authority to streamline the operation. He set up a system that staggered the distribution of food ration cards throughout the month instead of concentrating it at the beginning of every month. In the end, he employed three secretaries and from what I could observe on my occasional visits there, the distribution of the food ration cards was run efficiently and with minimum inconvenience for the many hundreds of family heads and individuals who had to travel often many miles to Vilkaviškis to receive their family's ration cards.

At first, it felt strange being back in Lithuania after almost two years in Germany where only German was spoken. This time Lithuanian Germans were no longer the underdogs but if anything at times even perceived by native Lithuanians to be arrogant occupiers of their country due to the policies of the German civilian authorities. Generally, as long as the German army was in charge of the initial occupation, Lithuanians did not feel badly treated. The German military personnel appeared to have behaved fairly decently in their relations with the Lithuanian natives except toward Jews and Poles, who suffered horrible persecution from the very start. Many thousands of Jews were killed in the early stages of the German invasion and the rest deported to city ghettoes. Poles were often displaced from their homes and were unwelcome to both Germans and Lithuanians. After civilian officials from the German Reich took over the administration of Lithuania, discrimination and incidents of harsh treatment of Lithuanian natives occurred fairly often. I myself had little direct contact with Lithuanians except when passing them on the street, occasionally buying something from a Lithuanian store or a farm family, and once going to a Lithuanian dentist to have a tooth pulled. Food was available to Germans in their own stores, where they used their ration cards. Lithuanians received lower rations than Germans. Most families, German and Lithuanian, tried to grow some vegetables including potatoes in a garden. Since Lithuania was primarily an agricultural country, there were some occasional shortages but few hardships due to lack of food.

When some of the German officials working in the offices near my dad's discovered that I spoke some Lithuanian, they recruited me as a translator on a few "missions" to homes of Lithuanians. Since I had not used or heard the Lithuanian language for two years, I did not feel confident translating accurately even the simpler things. But what made me especially uncomfortable was when I was told to inform two Lithuanian families that their houses or apartments were to be confiscated and they would have to move. Needless to say, I made myself as scarce as possible when I thought my translation "services" would again be needed.

After several months in the cramped living quarters of the German office building, my parents found a nice apartment in a one-story duplex within walking distance of my dad's office and the German elementary school that I attended. We felt lucky because it was not easy to find housing in Vilkaviškis, which had suffered much damage during the early days of the German invasion in June 1941. The Lithuanian owner of the house into which we moved occupied the next door apartment. At first, he did not seem to be enthusiastic to have Germans as neighbors but with time he warmed up and we had a good relationship. We heard rumors from other Lithuanians that our landlord had collaborated with the communists during the Soviet occupation and that he had leftist leanings. However, none of this became an issue with us. Our landlord was about the only Lithuanian whom my parents and I came to know well and had almost daily contact. We were even invited to an elaborate family celebration of the christening of his young son by his second wife, whom he had married after being widowed. All other Lithuanians were distant acquaintances. Once when my mother became friendly with one Lithuanian woman, she soon indicated that she had to be careful not to be seen much in the company of Germans, for some of her fellow Lithuanians held that against her.

Though our stay in the new home was to be short-lived, its inside brightened up and became more homelike when my parents were able to get our furniture sent from the storage facilities near Danzig, where it had been placed since our resettlement in early 1941. All of the furniture, household goods, dad's sizable book collection, and harmonium survived the move except a valuable heavy oak ward-robe closet which 'disappeared.' The apartment also had running water and an inside toilet unlike our dwelling in Pilviškiai. Outside our apartment we had a garden to grow a few vegetables and I kept a few rabbits in a shed in the yard as pets. Our stay in this comfort-able home lasted only a year and a half, for we were forced again to evacuate in July 1944 by the retreating eastern front line.

My main activities centered on school and Hitler Youth meet-ings, but I also had free time to myself and with friends. There were no church services or Sunday school meetings, neither of which I must say I missed. At home, my parents insisted on having regular family devotions on Sundays. A German elementary school began classes only a block or two away from our first residence within three months after our arrival. It was housed in a small building that had suffered some war damage and soon became crowded. Even though the teacher had to handle several levels of elementary class-es, she managed to provide a good basic instruction in most subjects. During classroom breaks some of us boys entertained ourselves by throwing large stones and bricks against a wall and a chimney of a nearby building that was still standing after most of the rest had collapsed in ruins. A small celebration followed when we finally got the chimney to topple. What surprises me is that no teacher or other adult interfered with our "game," and when we returned to the class-room there were no rebukes. Luckily no one got injured as far as I remember. Fortunately after about three months the school moved to a larger and more adequate facility, which had a large yard and served us well until all Germans had to evacuate.

The curriculum of my elementary school covered heavy doses of basic math, German, and history. We also had instruction in geography, beginning biology, and physical education. I enjoyed borrowing books, especially biographies and historical accounts, from the small school library. The teacher was a Lithuanian German, who had probably received some concentrated short term training, before she was allowed to enter a German classroom. There was a shortage of teachers in German schools in Lithuania during the occupation. In our school only the principal, who also served as the school superintendent of the county, was originally from Germany. He found little time to teach since his main charge was to administer the school system of the region of Vilkaviškis. He was the only school official who wore a brown uniform like many of the German civilian administrative officials. They were sometimes derisively called "golden pheasants." The principal-school superintendent did not show any overt leanings toward Nazism, just as my elementary teacher did not treat us to any blatant Nazi propaganda in the classroom. However, her slant of history reflected the emphases that were common in textbooks of Nazi Germany. Charlemagne, for instance, was extolled as a great Frankish leader but also chastised for having slaughtered too many Saxons, who were regarded to have been more Aryan and racially pure than most of his other enemies in Western Europe. The Nazi authorities also frowned on certain dramas of Germany's classical playwrights. Thus the showing of a film at our school of Friedrich Schiller's play, *Wilhelm Tell,* was given a fair amount of advance publicity but then unceremoniously canceled. The rebellious protagonist in the play, rising up against a tyrant, was found objectionable and too risky an example of a hero, even though other plays by the famous German playwright were considered acceptable to the Nazi authorities. Schoolteachers were at times also expected to be involved in Hitler Youth leadership activities, though none of mine in East Prussia and in Lithuania were.

In the spring 1944, after turning twelve, I was long overdue to change from elementary school to secondary school if I was to receive an academic education within the German school system rather than follow a vocational track. The decision to continue schooling of sons and daughters in a secondary school was usually made by the parents. However, not every elementary school student would qualify for secondary education. After the fourth grade of elementary school, students normally had to pass a high school entrance examination. I was already in the fifth elementary grade and had good grades, so I was not required to take a qualifying examination. There was no German secondary school in Vilkaviškis so I enrolled in the closest German high school located in Eydtkau (prewar Germany), right across from the Lithuanian border town of Kybartai, my birthplace. Two of my older cousins had previously attended this school. I was boarded with a widow friend of the family in Kybartai and walked across the border every weekday to attend school. Even though Lithuania was under German occupation, there was still a border checkpoint manned by German border guards. From time to time they would ask me and my fellow schoolmates to open our briefcases to make sure we were not smuggling something into Germany or out of it.

In the new school I had no difficulty keeping up with all subjects except English, the first required foreign language taught in most German secondary schools. The high school class that I entered had already had more than half a year of instruction in the English language and so I and several other German classmates from Lithuania had to take remedial lessons from a private tutor to catch up . The tutor was the younger of two elderly sisters. She suffered from epilepsy, but this did not interfere with her ability to give private lessons. When she had epileptic spells and passed out for a few minutes we only needed to call her sister, and our teacher soon recovered and then simply continued with us. Even though these lessons only lasted a few months until school adjourned for vacation, I got a good start in English and was able to continue later first with a tutor and then on my own. The two sisters asked for compensation in kind rather than money. They knew that we came from more rural areas and our families had more access to agricultural meat products like bacon, ham, or sausages than they had in a German city. This meant that several of us had to carry these products past the border check-point. Fortunately, we never got caught since the guards got used to seeing some of us crossing the border every weekday and treated us more and more like innocent schoolboys.

High school was my first time away from home for more than a short vacation, and I came to enjoy my freedom from immediate parental supervision. The lady I stayed with took care of my meals and was quite lenient in allowing me to wander about in Kybartai and visit with my classmates in the vicinity. Several of them had transferred from Vilkaviškis at about the same time as I had, and so I did not have to start with all new friends. The amount of school home-work was reasonable and left us quite a bit of free time for play. Some of our games during our leisure time were however not always harmless. Around nearby military barracks soldiers had carelessly dropped some rifle ammunition. One of my classmates showed the rest of us how to remove the slug from the bullet case and then to light the powder with a match. Sometimes we left the bullet inside the case after briefly removing it and then lit the powder to watch the bullet fly out of the case. Fortunately we never stumbled on any grenades, for the game with the bullets was risky enough. On Satur-days, after our morning classes, several of us took the public bus that passed through Kybartai to Vilkaviškis to spend the short weekend at home. On Sunday afternoons we returned to Kybartai by train. However, on at least two occasions when we needed the train to go back it was not operating because partisans had blown up some train tracks, tying to disrupt the German supply lines. This was always a reminder that we were living in wartime and Germans were facing not only an enemy on the still distant eastern front but also guerilla attacks on installations and persons behind the front line.

School and Hitler Youth

The Nazi government considered the education of the youth essential in its effort of instilling Nazi ideals into the German populace. Hitler especially expected the youth to become the core of the new national socialist community. Schools and the Hitler Youth organization were to win the young generation for nationalism, imbuing them with pride in their country and the Nationalist Socialist spirit and ideology. In practice schools did not always fulfill this role since the Nazi regime was only in power for twelve years, half of which comprised the war period. Communist, Socialist, and Jewish teachers were removed from their positions after Hitler came into power. German teachers were normally classified as civil servants and therefore subject to the regulations of the German civil service bureaucracy. Most teachers were under pressure to join the National Socialist Teachers Association, and by the end of the 1930s the overwhelming majority had done so. But not all members of the Nazi Teachers organization considered it important to inject Nazi ideology into the school curriculum. In my experience, they were generally devoted to educating young people by teaching their respective subjects without any particular emphasis on Nazi ideas.

Textbooks in my elementary school in Tilsit and later in secondary school in Eydtkau contained more explicit references to Nazi ideological ideas than what teachers actually presented in the classroom. History narratives followed a prescribed emphasis on the history of the Nazi movement and, for the earlier epochs, on the greatness of the German medieval empire, the colonization of eastern European territories by Germanic peoples, the rise of Prussia as a prelude to the German Empire. The objective was to extol the greatness of the German fatherland and the creative and heroic qualities of the German people. However, the classroom history lessons that I remember gave me much more an overview of historical events and personalities than their greatness. Geography readings would sometimes highlight Nazi geopolitical aspects, but in class we were taught the location of countries, rivers, mountains, and cities rather than their political significance. Similarly in biology the study of races was to be an important component, but it was not well covered by my teachers in their class presentations. They were more interested in telling us about plants, animals, and humans than the characteristics of human races.

The Nazi leadership expected to inculcate its ideals to the fullest into German youth through the Hitler Youth. Here my own association with the *Jungvolk* (Young Folk), the ten-to-fourteen-year-old-boys' formation of the actual Hitler Youth, illustrates the Nazi youth indoctrination. The Hitler Youth organization originated in the 1920s when the Nazi party was a struggling political movement. When Adolf Hitler rose to power in 1933, all political parties and labor unions were dissolved. Youth organizations, except for a few religious youth groups, were also dissolved or reorganized. The National Socialist German Workers' Party or Nazi party became the only legitimate political party and took under its control many of the reorganized associations that reached out into other parts of German society. In 1936 the Hitler Youth became a "Supreme Governmental Authority" and was subordinated directly to Hitler. Even though its ranks swelled very substantially after 1933, membership for all German boys ten years or older (and girls in the parallel Young Girls' formation) became compulsory only in 1939.

In a speech at the Nuremberg Party Rally in 1935, Hitler declared that the National Socialist youth of the future must be "slim and slender, swift as the greyhound, tough as leather, and hard as Krupp steel." These character traits were to be fostered through the activities of the Hitler Youth, many of which resembled the activities of any kind of youth organization with arts and crafts, building model air planes and ships, group singing, camping, and sports. Superficially, to some the Hitler Youth program might have appeared to be that of the forbidden Boy Scouts, augmented with more intensive patriotism and militaristic elements. In reality the dynamic of Hitler Youth activities was different from other youth groups, stressing competitiveness and ideology. The top leadership of the Hitler Youth was in the hands of adults who were part of a bureaucratized enterprise and only the lower echelons had leaders drawn from the younger ranks, following the principle of 'youth leads youth.' Much emphasis was placed on competition and achievement, especially in sports. We had to participate in numerous athletic events in which we were tested for speed in running, the length of leaps in broad jumps, throwing of shot puts or occasionally javelins, individually and as a group. Those who excelled earned different badges. I hated these athletic competitions since I was never good at any of these pursuits. Since leadership advancement went with prowess in athletics, I would have never made it far in the Hitler Youth. I could compete with my peers intellectually, but could not successfully compete in athletic achievement. More amenable to me were the occasional soccer games, which involved teamwork and had a recreational aspect.

The ideological conditioning of the youth in accordance with National Socialist ideals extolled ardent patriotism, duty, obedience, honor, courage, selfless devotion to Germany, and absolute loyalty to Adolf Hitler. The motto of the Hitler Youth was, "Führer command -- we follow!" This idea was to be imparted through quasi military activities. While I lived in Vilkaviškis most of our weekly meetings were held on either Saturday afternoons or Sunday mornings, sometimes both. Almost all of our meetings began with roll calls where we reported like soldiers for duty. Then there was much marching and more than enough drill, some military like games, singing of songs that had as themes the flag, honor, the fatherland, comradeship, heroism, and willingness to die in battle. The most important Nazi song that we had to know by heart was the Hitler Youth anthem: "Vorwärts, vorwärts schmettern die hellen Fanfaren" with one very telling line: "Ja, die Fahne ist mehr als der Tod" (Forward, forward the fanfares blare; yes, the flag rates higher than death).

Training manuals that were to inform our ideological sessions highlighted the life of Adolf Hitler, his humble origin, his courageous war service, his building of the Nazi movement, and its achievement in toppling the Weimar "system." Under Hitler, Germany overcame the perceived unfair and disgraceful dictate of the Versailles treaty of 1919 and embarked on a path to greatness. Other aspects emphasized the superiority of the Aryan race and its destiny of ruling the world. Nazi ideology singled out the Jews as particular "Staatsfeinde" (enemies of the state) in its twisted concoction of racial theory, in addition to Communists, Social Democrats, Gypsies, homosexuals, Freemasons, and Jehova's Witnesses. In the Hitler Youth sessions that I attended first in Tilsit and later in Vilkaviškis, the Jews and the other "enemies of the state" were given little attention. But when I perused a training manual, I found this very subject was quite prominently covered there.

On special days like Hitler's birthday, April 20, we had rallies that brought together units of the Hitler Youth from several neighboring communities of Vilkaviškis for parades and ceremonial events. Common uniforms were supposed to help build the notion of one national community in which class differences had been overcome. War conditions made it difficult for our parents to buy complete uniforms because of shortages. As a result, a good many of us had only partial uniform pieces, and thus we did not present the most impressive image of national uniformity. Another memorable event was attending a weeklong Hitler Youth camp at a lake near the southwest border of prewar Lithuania. Together with several youths from the same home unit I joined a hundred or so boys from communities in the wider Vilkaviškis area in the summer of 1943. It was an interesting experience, but for me not very enjoyable. We slept in regular housing together with a group of boys, most of them strangers. Here and there I ran into three of my cousins who had come from Pilviškiai. In the morning and in the afternoon we spent a lot of time on cross-country runs and even more on calisthenics. Some of these activities were planned but some of them were merely punishment for one infraction or another. In addition there were marching and drill. All of this exhausted us physically and left little time for swimming in the lake, instruction sessions, and campfires in the evening.

My service in the Hitler Youth was relatively short-lived. After I transferred to the secondary school in Eydtkau, I could no longer attend all of the mandatory meetings in Vilkaviškis. When months later we had to evacuate Lithuania and found a temporary home in West Prussia, I briefly resumed my affiliation with a Jungvolk unit in Zuckau. But conditions were becoming disorganized as the German forces retreated under the pressure of the Soviet armies, and Hitler Youth meetings ended. My only constructive contributions in the service of the Hitler Youth, and this largely under school auspices, were to collect donations for the party sponsored Winter Relief organization in Vilkaviškis and, during our stay in West Prussia, to help bring in the potato harvest.

Did my association with the Hitler Youth turn me into a believing Nazi? Hardly. Even though I was proud to be a German and identified with the strong German Reich that reached beyond Germany's prewar borders, I did not anticipate the brutal expansion of German domination into Russia about which we were taught very little. It was reassuring that German armies controlled much of Central and Western Europe and that Germany was playing a major role in European international politics. I recognized Hitler as the leader of Germany and felt he had accomplished much in restoring Germany's might after he came into power in 1933. I also hoped that Germany would indeed win the war. Even though I accepted the Nazi dictum of becoming a loyal follower of the leaders under whom I served and fulfilling my duty in whatever position I was placed, the Nazi values of racial superiority, suppression of non-Aryans, exploitation and elimination of all those that the regime deemed inferior or worthless did not become a conscious part of my mental and emotional attitude toward others. Here my Christian upbringing at home militated against a blind acceptance of Nazi ideology, for my parents were no German patriots let alone National Socialists. Had they been believing adherents of the Third Reich, my attitudinal outlook might well have been different.

While I observed the painful discrimination against Jews in Germany and heard of the existence of concentration camps for dissenters and opponents of the Nazi regime and the murder of Jews in Lithuania, these did not yet lead me to conclude that the Hitler regime itself was totally evil. This realization came to me only after the defeat of Germany and the full revelations of the Nuremberg Trial in 1945 and 1946, which made widely known the brutal exploitation of the conquered territories and the systematic murder of millions of Jews, Poles, Russians, and many other Eastern Europeans by the Nazis.

I remember how my father showed courage and indirectly expressed some dissent when at a birthday party for him at our home to which his office staff and other German officials and their staffs had been invited, he opened the occasion with a prayer. In the course of the conversation, while the guests were enjoying coffee and cake, one of the more fanatical young Lithuanian German staff members exclaimed that once the war had been won this would bring the end of the Christian churches. Though not formally proclaimed in public, this was indeed Hitler's intention, as he had been angered by expressions of dissent and protest by both Lutheran and Catholic Church leaders against Nazi policies. Parenthetically, the young outspoken Nazi believer was drafted into the army months later and soon died on the front lines.

The German Occupation of Lithuania

When the German armies stormed into the Baltic States on June 22, 1941, they were often greeted as liberators from the hated Soviet occupiers. During the week preceding the German invasion, the Soviets deported many tens of thousands of Estonians, Latvians, and Lithuanians to an uncertain fate into the interior of Russia. It is estimated that over 34,000 Lithuanians were arrested and sent in boxcars eastward between June 14 and 18 (Misiunas and Taagepera 42). Many more would have followed if it had not been for the sudden advance of the German armed forces, which reached and occupied Kaunas in three days. The average Lithuanian hoped that the overthrow of the Soviet regime would lead to the restoration of Lithuanian independence. In fact, a group of Lithuanian insurgents who helped drive the Soviet troops out of Kaunas even before the German forces arrived proclaimed the reestablishment of Lithuanian independence and the creation of a Provisional Government. However, German plans for the occupation of Lithuania did not include granting her independence or even autonomy. Whereas the German military administration worked around the six-week Lithuanian Provisional Government, the German civilian authorities upon assuming control of Lithuania simply appointed Germans to leading positions in the administration and economy of the state without regard to already named Lithuanians.

It was in the early days of the German campaign into Russia that the first violent actions against Lithuanian Jews were unleashed. Many Lithuanians believed the allegation against Jews that they had welcomed the Soviet intervention and had widely participated in the communist administration that oppressed the native population and perpetrated the arrest and deportation of many of their countrymen. It is true the number of Lithuanian Jews who held positions in the communist Lithuanian government was proportionally higher than the total number of Jews living in Lithuania. However, when it came to victimizing Lithuanians and deporting many of them to the Soviet Union, Jews were also represented among the deportees. These individuals were singled out for removal like the rest of the Lithuanians who were suspect in the eyes of the communist regime because of their social class origins or positions in pre-communist Lithuanian government and society. Some of the deportees were denounced to the communist authorities by their local enemies. Mobs of the population, who acted out their anticommunist revenge in Kaunas and several places in Lithuania when the German invasion began, vented their violence against the innocent Jewish population and massacred hundreds of them. Within days after the initial occupation of the country, a special German task force or *Einsatzgruppe*, separate from the German military, initiated large-scale murder actions against Lithuanian communists and especially Jews, resulting in the death of thousands of Lithuanian Jews in the months that followed. By October 1941 almost a third of the 200,000 Lithuanian Jews had been murdered. The rest were sent to ghettoes, the largest of which were in Kaunas and Vilnius, where they were forced to endure miserable living and working conditions. Those Jews who survived in the ghettoes were later shipped to death camps in Poland. It is estimated that about 170,000 Jews of Lithuania perished in the Holocaust (Misiunas and Taagepera 64), but most Germans and non-Germans did not learn about the large numbers until after the war.

When Aunt Olga Reinert returned to her farm in Lithuania in 1942 she heard from her neighbors what had happened to the Jews in Pilviškiai during the early weeks of the German occupation. She related some details to my dad in a conversation, which I happened to overhear. I was especially struck to learn what became of several of the Jews in Pilviškiai whom I knew personally. Our own physician and his son, who was somewhat older than I, were shot in the immediate days of the German invasion. His wife, who had been our dentist and her daughter survived the first onslaught, but suffered an uncertain and unknown fate. Several other Jewish acquaintances also did not survive. During my time in Lithuania I only heard about the Kaunas ghetto from a relative when my mother and I visited the city in the summer of 1943.

Native Lithuanians were disappointed quite early when the German authorities refused to restore Soviet-confiscated private property to their original owners, as most Lithuanians had expected. This was done only in limited instances and not until almost the end of the German occupation. The ultimate plans of the Nazi leadership to Germanize all of the Baltic States, which included the planned deportation of 85% of the Lithuanians, were carefully kept secret. Still, the civilian occupation authorities under Theodor Adrian von Renteln, the General Commissioner for Lithuania, launched a policy of relentless exploitation of economic and manpower resources of Lithuania for Germany's war time effort. Germans had special rights in Lithuania and natives were relegated to second class status. Food rations of Lithuanians were lower than those of Germans and the wage and price structure was skewed in Germany's favor. Cultural life was one area that was less affected by German discriminatory policy. Lithuanian theater, the arts, and musical performances like the opera were functioning as well as they could under the restraints of wartime conditions. Educational and religious affairs were controlled but not subjected to significant ideological regimentation, even though they suffered as a result of the manpower mobilization efforts. The universities of Kaunas and Vilnius opened in the fall of 1941, but were closed in early 1943 when German authorities felt thwarted in their efforts to recruit Lithuanian men for their army (Misiunas and Taagepera 54).

Lithuanian antagonism toward the occupying regime intensified as German demands for contributions in products and manpower increased and harsh measures enforced these demands. Lithuanian farmers were required to deliver agricultural products at set quotas. If deliveries were not met or machinery broke down, there was the suspicion of deliberate sabotage for which severe punishment was meted out. I remember one of the German officials in charge of overseeing agricultural deliveries in the Vilkaviškis area, whom I came to know fairly well, caused the execution of a Lithuanian farm laborer for sabotage of farm machinery. However, when later investigation established that this man was innocent.

As early as July 1941, a sizable number of Lithuanians were recruited for voluntary farm labor in East Prussia. When reports came back that many of them were being treated like prisoners and even beaten, voluntary enlistment plummeted and the German authorities resorted to repressive measures in conscripting Lithuanian workers for Germany. In December 1941 a general work obligation was decreed for those aged 18 to 45. As many potential workers continued to evade the recruitment and went underground or took to the woods, the German authorities adopted even more drastic methods. Members of the Lithuanian intelligentsia were arrested and sent to the concentration camp of Stutthof near Danzig. Starting in the fall of 1943, German authorities at times surrounded churches on Sunday mornings during a regular service and arrested able-bodied men and some women for deportation to the Reich. By early 1944 close to 75,000 Lithuanians had been taken to Germany and forced to work in the armaments industry (Misiunas and Taagepera 56). Once when several German soldiers had been murdered by partisans, German forces exacted revenge by killing hundreds of Lithuanian villagers, even though the acts of murder had most likely been committed by Soviet rather than Lithuanian partisans (Stossun 215). The harsh labor recruitment policies and isolated instances of mass revenge could not help but sour the relations between the Lithuanian populace and the German occupiers. In contrast, it is striking that the relations between Lithuanians and the German resettlers remained relatively peaceful. There were few attacks on Lithuanian German

farmers and civilians. However, my parents and I found that Lithuanians generally kept aloof from close relations with Germans for
fear of incurring the hostility of their own people.

Given the unhappy state of formal Lithuanian-German relations,
it was not surprising that German efforts to bolster their military
force with Lithuanian recruits largely failed. The Lithuanian prewar army which had been transformed into a Soviet military unit
surrendered very quickly after the German attack in the summer of
1941. Most of these men were then recruited under German auspices for Defense Battalions. Even though these battalions were to
be stationed for duty in their homeland, they were soon used behind the German eastern front lines and some of them in Poland
for guard duty or population control and anti-guerilla operations. In
1942 and 1943 the Germans created Waffen-SS National Legions
but succeeded only in forming Estonian and Latvian units; most
draft worthy Lithuanians refused service and by March 1943 were
considered unworthy to wear the SS uniform (Misiunas and Taagepera 58). Thus few Lithuanian soldiers came to serve in the German
front lines in defense of Germany or their own homeland. In the
late spring and summer 1944 the retreating eastern front reached the
Lithuanian border. The German retreat foreboded the coming flight
westward of Germans and quite a fair number of frightened Lithuanians as well as the advancing Soviet armies relentlessly pushed
the German armed forces toward eventual defeat.

References

Misiunas, Ramuald J., and Rein Taagepera. *The Baltic States:
Years of Dependence 1940-1990*. Expanded and updated ed. Berkeley and Los Angeles: University of California Press, 1993.

Stossun, Harry. *Die Umsiedlungen der Deutschen aus Litauen
während des Zweiten Weltkrieges*. Marburg/Lahn: J.G. Herder Institut, 1993

FIVE

Flight Back to Germany

Evacuation to West Prussia

Two turning points in the war left an indelible mark in my memory during our short-lived time in German-occupied Lithuania: the Stalingrad disaster in early 1943, which signaled the turn of the tide against Germany on the eastern front, and the Allied invasion of Normandy in early June 1944, presaging the beginning of the end for Germany's war in Europe. The first event came at the beginning of our return to German-occupied Lithuania and the second when we were already wondering how many more weeks were left before we would be forced to leave our home again.

As related earlier, after our return to Lithuania most of us concentrated on getting settled and starting as normal a life as was possible under conditions that showed no immediately threatening effects of the war. Unlike many cities in western Germany which were experiencing Allied bombing raids, we were spared these frequent reminders of how costly the war could be to civilians. Even though the German armies in 1941 had been halted before the gates of Moscow by the unusually bitter winter and by the temporarily recovered Soviet forces, who staged short-lived offensives in December 1941 and January 1942, the German armies were able to resume the campaign into the interior of Soviet Russia in the spring of 1942. They seemingly rolled triumphantly eastward during the summer and early fall. Hitler hoped to end the war on the eastern front during that year by conquering some the most important agricultural and industrial resource areas of Russia, including the coveted oil fields of the Caucasus, and thereby forcing the Soviet government into defeat.

As a ten- year-old I was in 1942 not yet a regular newspaper reader except when some unusual events or occurrences were being reported. Since at that point my parents did not own a radio, German newspapers were our principal news source about our new surroundings, the war, and Germany. When I picked up our daily newspaper around the second or third of February 1943, the bold front page headline announced that the German Sixth Army at Stalingrad had been destroyed after "heroic resistance." Even the censored military news did not disguise the fact that the Battle of Stalingrad, which raged from mid-November 1942 to the last day of January 1943, had ended in the annihilation of an entire German army that fought in a besieged city to the bitter end.

Stalingrad marked the farthest advance of the German forces into Russia and their terribly costly defeat in the city named after the Soviet dictator in power set an end to any further German territorial expansion into the Soviet Union during the remaining eastern campaign. Interestingly, perhaps in part because of the thousand-mile distance from Lithuania, the bitter Stalingrad defeat of the German armies did not arouse any alarm among Germans in the Baltic States. However, the German military disaster at Stalingrad not only turned Hitler's hope into a ghostly dream, but its aftermath made it glaringly evident that the German military could no longer launch sustained offensives against the Red Army. By drawing on vast Soviet manpower reserves, revitalized war production, and Lend Lease aid from the Americans, Germany's eastern opponent had grown stronger in numbers of men and armor, exceeding the capacity of the already smaller German forces to restore their losses.

In the first half of 1943 and beyond, German government propaganda continued to trumpet the lie that the retreating front lines in Russia were due to "strategic withdrawals," not defeat. This official attitude was convincing to many if not most Germans in Lithuania and in the Reich, and helped sustain the hope that as long as the eastern front was far away in the depths of Russia, Germany would in the end prevail victoriously in the war. But early in July 1943, the German armies suffered another very costly military setback during the gigantic tank battle at Kursk, only five hundred miles from the German border. By mobilizing 2700 tanks and a significant infantry concentration, Hitler launched the last major attack of the war against the Red Army in the center of the eastern front. Stalin mustered an even larger number of tanks and support forces and, despite heavy losses, stopped the German offensive in its tracks. The Russians recovered from their losses at Kursk but the German losses in tanks and assault guns were so heavy that Hitler's armies were no longer able to launch major attacks against the advancing Soviets. From thereon the German armies were forced into a permanent retreat, though they still at times fought bitter defensive battles that were costly to both sides. In the spring of 1944 they were dislodged from the western Ukraine and during the ensuing season had to abandon all Soviet Russian territories and withdraw into eastern and central Poland. When the Red Army began to push the German front lines closer to the borders of the Baltic States in the late spring and early summer of 1944, it became clear that Germans would not be able to stay in Lithuania much longer.

While we were anxiously anticipating the months ahead of us, on June 1, my paternal grandmother died at the age of 89. She had not been well for quite a few months. In retrospect, we marveled how her passing came so very timely, sparing her all the hardships of the flight that soon followed. Only six weeks later the relatives in Pilviškiai were ordered to evacuate Her funeral served as a family reunion before the turbulent war conditions scattered all of us on our flight from the retreating eastern front lines. My Uncle Karl Blum and his wife Ottilie and Aunt Alma Schulz, who now were established in West Prussia, were also able to attend the funeral. My grandmother was buried in the same cemetery as my Aunt Olga's husband, Uncle Gustav Reinert. He had donated a plot of land from his farmland to the Pilviškiai Methodist Church, and had died all too early of cancer in 1937. Since Germans during the German occupation were not allowed to hold public church services in Lithuania, my grandmother's funeral service at the cemetery was held without official permission. A second cousin of my dad's, who was an ordained Methodist minister but was not active in church work during the war years, presided at the funeral. He spoke in German and my dad addressed the Lithuanian neighbors and friends of my grandmother in their language. After the Germans were forced to flee from Lithuania, the cemetery fell into disarray for several decades. Some of my German cousins visited their parents' farm and their hometown once in the late 1980s, under the Soviets, and several times in the early 1990s after Lithuania had regained its independence. With the help of the immediate family, the graves of my grandmother and Uncle Gustav were restored and appropriate tombstones were added. They found that no buildings of the two adjoining family farms survived he war and almost all of the once fertile and productively cultivated land had turned into a steppe.

Immediately after my grandmother's funeral, I returned to Kybartai to continue school for several more weeks. A few days later, while on my morning walk to school from Kybartai to Eydtkau, I learned of the Normandy Invasion from the newspaper headlines at a kiosk. It began on June 6, 1944, and the next day the local German newspaper announced in bold black letters: "The Invasion has begun." At the time, German propaganda had created the expectation in the public that the Allied invaders of France would be thrown back into the Channel and that the German defense line of the "Atlantic Wall" was impenetrable. However, when the Western Allied forces gained a quick foothold on the Normandy coast and then began to push into the interior of France, the realities on the French battle fields starkly belied the boastful claims of the German propaganda. It was dangerous to express any doubts about German victory, as the pronouncements of the Joseph Goebbels Propaganda

Ministry confidently continued to predict, to anyone except trusted family and friends. Doubters and dissenters could be denounced to the Nazi authorities by whoever overheard them and then punished as defeatists if not traitors. But as the war progressed without German victories, more and more Germans were losing hope that Germany could still win the war. In my family we did not talk much about that, but my parents and I had for some time begun to believe that a German victory was unattainable. For us it was now a matter of how and whether we would survive during the months and years to come. Even though the Allied invasion of France boded more ill for the overall German war effort, we in the Baltic area were much more concerned about how long the German defense lines in the East would withstand the relentless pressure of the advancing Soviet forces in the summer of 1944.

On June 22, 1944, the third anniversary of the German attack on the Soviet Union and a few weeks after the Normandy invasion started, the Red Army launched a big offensive on the eastern front. The Soviet forces smashed through German Army Group Center within days and created a huge breach in the entire eastern front. German military losses were enormous and enabled the Red Army to drive through the pulverized German defense lines for hundreds of miles. By the end of July Soviet troops reached the eastern outskirts of Warsaw and captured two bridgeheads on the Vistula River in central Poland. Farther north in Lithuania, Vilnius fell to the Soviets on July 13 and Kaunas by the end of the month.

Most of the German civilians were ordered to leave Vilkaviškis several days after Vilnius, less than 90 miles away, was overrun by Soviet troops. School in Eydtkau adjourned for summer vacation in the second half of June, and I had returned home to be with my parents awaiting the coming developments. For more than a week before our evacuation from that area we could hear the distant thunder of heavy guns.

The order for German civilians to clear out of Vilkaviškis came around July 15. Within a day or so my father was able to find a horse-drawn wagon that carried us and some of our belongings, including a few pieces of furniture, to Kybartai, where we found a temporary shelter at the small apartment of our family friend with whom I had stayed while attending secondary school in Eydtkau. Fortunately, our friend had been planning to evacuate about the time when we arrived so that neither she nor we were inconvenienced when we crowded into her home. We did not expect to stay in Kybartai very long, however, for the eastern front line did not appear to be holding well enough to assure that. With concern we waited from day to day, watching for news on new developments. On our small radio, we received regular national news reports. Otherwise we kept in touch with the local German civilian administration during our two-week stay in Kybartai.

On July 20, in the evening, came the startling radio announcement that an attempt had been made on Hitler's life at his headquarters in East Prussia. It failed when the Führer escaped practically unharmed, even though several members of his staff died or were injured when a bomb went off during a military staff conference. Hitler took savage revenge on the "clique of military officers" (and civilian leaders), as they were branded in official Nazi pronouncements, who had conspired to remove the Führer from power and initiate negotiations with the Allies to end the war. At the time, my father remarked that Hitler's survival probably prevented the outbreak of chaos throughout Germany. It was not until after the war that I learned the particulars of the opposition against Hitler and the motives of its members. The prospects of replacing the Nazi rulers with a non-Nazi government were by no means assured even if Hitler had been killed in the attempt. However, more than likely even under Nazi leadership, headed by someone like Hermann Göring (Hitler's designated successor), the fanatical pursuit of the war to the final destruction of Germany would have ended, saving thereby many hundreds of thousands of lives on both sides.

The remaining days in Kybartai were made more troublesome for us when my mother fell in our temporary apartment and broke her left wrist, leaving her with a painful handicap in the weeks ahead. A military doctor put her arm in a cast without properly aligning the fractured bone, which left her with a permanently misaligned left wrist, since it was impossible to get proper medical care until weeks later. About a week after my mother's mishap the order came to evacuate Kybartai within a day, and we hastily departed from Lithuania on July 31. In fact, the German occupation of Lithuania ended sooner than many of us had anticipated and when my parents and I left our short-lived new home we became refugees.

On a small horse-drawn wagon, which my father was able to borrow for a few hours, we transported our reduced possessions to the station, where an evacuation train was waiting. This time we were only allowed to take clothes, some bedding, and a few necessary household goods. The furniture and trunks with my dad's books as well as most household goods that we had saved so far had to be left behind. The loading of the train with evacuees and their possessions began in the morning but the departure of the train was delayed by quite a few hours; it was suddenly expedited when a Soviet air raid threatened the train station. Fortunately, apart from being briefly strafed by several hostile airplanes, which fired a few random shots, the train pulled out of the station in the late afternoon without suffering any damage.

After we had boarded the passenger car to which we had been directed, some of us discovered that right behind our train car a freight car had been placed with discarded military articles, including rifles, rifle ammunition but, worst of all, also several land mines and hand grenades. Having this unwelcome load of potential explosives right behind our train car made our trip so much more hazardous in case of an attack from the air or a train accident. We were not given a specific destination for our train journey except that we were to be resettled somewhere in West Prussia. The trip itself was uneventful and in the afternoon of the next day, August 1, the train stopped and unloaded most of the evacuees in Zuckau, a small town about 15 miles southwest of Danzig (today Gdansk).

In the first week of August Soviet forces advanced as far as Vilkaviškis but were thrown back by repeated German counterattacks, which temporarily stabilized the front lines in that region. However, most of the town in which we had lived for over a year and a half was left in ruins by the fierce fighting. The evacuation from Kybartai had been fairly well organized by the German authorities and so were also our arrival and transportation to a new home. At the Zuckau station we were met by drivers with horse drawn-wagons, who consulted lists to distribute the new refugees largely among local farmer families for their housing. My parents and I were assigned to a forester family home, some seven miles away from Zuckau. The family who had been ordered to take in newcomers turned out to be friendly. They had a large enough house to accommodate additional residents and the rooms that we were given were quite nice and certainly adequate for us. In addition to the parents, there were a young teen-age son and a daughter, who also fairly quickly opened up to me and eased my adjustment in the new surroundings. However, the distinct drawback of our new location was the distance from the nearby town, where I would be attending school and where my father would expect to find some employment.

After obtaining ration cards and attending to the required registration with the local authorities, my parents began to press for a transfer to Zuckau. The main problem was finding housing. After some delay a room became available in the residence of an estate owner. It was rather dark and not very spacious, having probably served as the maid's or servant's quarters in better times. There were no kitchen facilities in the room and my mother had to compete for a place at the cooking stove in the family kitchen with a friendly German-speaking Polish maid and a vexatious German lady of the house while we lived there.

Once we were settled in our new small living accommodation, life returned to some normality. My father volunteered his book-keeping services to a mill owner at a short distance from our new home, which soon became his short-lived regular employment. In early September I returned to secondary school and also continued with private English lessons, given by an elderly teacher in the community. One of the school activities required me and my school-mates to help with the harvesting of potatoes during the early fall. The Hitler Youth troop in town, whose meetings I was obligated to attend, lacked good leadership. My school teacher had been assigned the responsibility to oversee Hitler Youth activities in addition to be-ing overburdened with teaching duties. Unfortunately for her, there were no effective leaders among the older youths of the troop to give direction and enforce discipline. As a result, meetings often became rather rowdy with little if anything being accomplished. After a few weeks the Hitler Youth meetings were discontinued. School contin-ued longer and adjourned for Christmas vacation in the second half of December, but did not reopen in January because there was fear that Germans might have to evacuate Zuckau.

Even with all the uncertainty about the future, those of us who were younger managed to enjoy some carefree activities in our free time. Several of my schoolmates whom I knew from my time in Kybartai had ended up in Zuckau, and we met from time to time to swim in a nearby river or just for usual fun. I also became friends with several local boys in the neighborhood. With one or two of them I took train trips to Karthaus, the county seat about ten miles away, and to Danzig, the most important and largest city of West Prussia. On a school sponsored excursion I had a chance to attend my very first opera, *Hänsel and Gretel*, at a theater in Danzig. It was not a regular production with adult opera singers but talented older children, accompanied by a piano rather than an orchestra. The performance aroused my interest in classical opera that I pursued in the years after the war. In the late fall and early winter, when the first snow fell, I tried some cross-country skiing. The German military were selling surplus skis at a very affordable price and this gave some of us a chance to obtain otherwise unavailable sports goods. While merrily skiing down a hill I landed in a plowed field and twisted my right knee, a reminder that this sport was not without hazards. A nearby creek had enough frozen ice to serve as a small ice rink for skating. At first I did not have skates but one day in December a package arrived from Aunt Alma Schulz. With her son's skates was a note which related that Alfons, my cousin only five years older than I, had died on the western front. I carried my cousin's skates with me on the next stages of our flight as long as I could, but in the end I had to leave them behind. A few days before Christmas, my cousin Albin Reinert suddenly appeared at our door. He was stationed nearby in the military and had been given a few days' leave after some strenuous military maneuvers. He stayed with us for only two days and then had to return to his unit. We did not see him again until two years later in Wollbach, Bavaria, when he came by for a short visit. He was fortunate to survive the war, but he lost his right leg during the last months of the war and had a prolonged bout with TB.

Throughout the fall and early winter of 1944 we were hearing mostly news about German military retreats on the eastern and the western fronts. In the East the Soviet forces had reached the borders of East Prussia, penetrated into Poland as far as Warsaw, and taken much of the Danube valley by the late summer and fall of 1944. The rapid advances of the Soviet forces still encountered fierce German resistance from time to time, which forced them to halt their offensive in the last months of 1944. After amassing more troops and materiel, the Red Army mounted its final assault on Germany in early 1945. On the western front, after breaking out from Normandy and following a second Allied landing in the south of France in August, the Allied American, British, and now also some French forces gained fairly steady ground in their liberation of France, Belgium, and the Netherlands. Toward the end of August they liberated Paris and by the end of October American troops occupied Aachen, the first German city. Yet German resistance did not abate and the Allies did not reach the Rhine until March1945.

Morale among the German populace remained high throughout 1944 despite intensified Anglo-American bombing raids on German cities in west and central Germany and the news of retreating German forces on all fronts: eastern, western, and southern in Italy. The German ground forces and the Luftwaffe were obviously no longer able to ensure a sustained defense of the German Reich against all its foes in the air and on land. So what hope was there that Germany's fortunes in the war could be turned from a dreaded defeat to a victorious end or at least a stalemate? Goebbels' propaganda machine tried to keep hope alive by claiming that Hitler's arsenal of arms contained secret wonder weapons which at crucial junctures were to achieve the turnabout. That summer the V-1, a flying bomb, was inaugurated and in the fall the V-2, a long range missile. Both of these very new weapons were deployed primarily against London and selectively against Allied forces on the continent. They caused considerable damage where they landed and killed a good many English civilians, but, apart from exacerbating fear among civilians, they did not achieve any kind of decisive breakthrough. Their limited effect was noted by many Germans, but Nazi propaganda persisted in spreading rumors that other secret wonder weapons would become available and turn the tide in Germany's favor. It is true that the German war machine had developed a limited number of early jet airplanes and new submarines. But the rapidly shrinking fuel and oil supplies kept these new weapons from becoming fully operational and also greatly limited the use of the existing airplanes and tanks in everyday combat. Due to fuel shortages airplane pilots did not get the kind of training they needed to be effective in action. So those diehards who still trusted the Führer to find some kind of weapon or strategy to save Germany from defeat were engaged in a wishful fantasy.

In mid-December 1944 came the astonishing announcement that the German armies had launched a great offensive against the Allied forces in Belgium and Luxembourg. This became the famous Battle of the Bulge in the Ardennes, a difficult terrain through which German tank formations had driven into France in their march to victory in 1940. It was Hitler's idea to strike unexpectedly with superior tank and infantry forces at a weak point of the enemy lines. The attack was begun during bad weather to prevent the Anglo-Americans from using their airplanes. The objective of the operation was to advance to the city-port of Antwerp and to split the British forces in the north from the American front lines in the south. To assure an overwhelming victory in the Ardennes offensive, Hitler even weakened German armor strength on the eastern front. He hoped the strike against the Western Allies would be decisive enough to enable him to end the war in the West and then withdraw large military formations to deploy them against the Soviets in the East. After suffering heavy losses, the Allied forces were temporarily driven back in several areas, but the Americans recovered and checked the German advances by the close of December. The German tanks were soon hampered by fuel shortages and became very vulnerable when the weather cleared and the Allies made full use of their airplanes in attacking tanks and troops. The German side suffered irreparable losses and, unlike the Allies, had no more reserves left to pursue Hitler's grand delusion of achieving a critical turnabout in the war.

While much hard fighting remained on both sides in the West and the devastating bombing of cities in central and western Germany persisted, for us in West Prussia it was of much greater concern what was happening in the East. Here the Red Army was mobilizing for its last assault on Hitler's crumbling Reich. This effort coincided with the American, British, and French drives into Germany from the west. On January 12, 1945, a little over two weeks after the Western Allies had gained the upper hand in the Battle of the Bulge, the Soviet armies mounted a massive attack against the German front lines in the region south of Warsaw. Three spearheads tore through the German front, driving toward East Prussia and Danzig to the north, into Warsaw and toward Poznan in the center, and toward Silesia in the southwest. While some of the Soviet thrusts were contained for a while by German resistance, the drive in the center rolled rapidly westward and reached Küstrin on the Oder by January 30, about 40 miles from the outskirts of Berlin. A few days earlier Russian tanks threatened Elbing, a city 60 miles east of Zuckau, and succeeded in isolating the German defense forces of East Prussia from those of West Prussia. The Russian advance toward the Oder created a wedge with a long, vulnerable northern flank, leaving most of the province of eastern Pomerania between the Soviet lines and the Baltic Sea in German hands. It was not until a month later that the Red Army was able to overcome some of the strong German resistance and occupy Pomerania and the rest of the territory east of the Oder River and west of the Vistula.

On the eve of the Soviet January offensive, we observed how the signs of war were getting more acute in our very region. The town of Zuckau had to accommodate hundreds of new refugees, exacerbating the local housing shortage and forcing more people into crowded dwellings. Danzig, the largest city near us, experienced only minor bombing before the fall but in the winter was struck hard by several Anglo-American bombing attacks. I remember how on two nights we watched from Zuckau the sky lit up and repeatedly heard the detonation of bombs falling on the city of Danzig. By this time, my parents and I no longer ventured into the city to avoid getting caught in a surprise air raid. Danzig suffered its worst destruction several months later during heavy fighting in the city and when Soviet troops even demolished some areas in the city after the war had already swept over it.

In the second half of January 1945, we appeared to be facing the imminent Russian invasion. Refugees fleeing from areas farther east were passing through Zuckau, but not staying. One of my parents' acquaintances, a German physician originally from Lithuania, together with his wife and sister-in-law stayed with us overnight, while they were on their way westward in their small car. They had made a narrow escape from Elbing after Soviet tanks were approaching the city limits. One evening, a disheartening sight for me was watching a column of emaciated concentration camp inmates, consisting of different nationalities, being driven through the town on a snowy night. For many of these poor people it must have been a death march. Such sights were a stark reminder for us that we had to do whatever we could to get out of West Prussia, which at that point was inhabited by a majority of Germans but also contained a strong minority of Poles. Once the tide turned against the Germans, many Poles could be expected to take their revenge on any German after having been oppressed and mistreated by the Nazi regime following the defeat of Poland in 1939.

Whereas the evacuation of the Germans from Lithuania in the summer of 1944 had been planned, there was no plan or preparation for an orderly evacuation of the German civilians from West Prussia. In fact, evacuation was either discouraged or sometimes forbidden by the Nazi party administration. Individual families had to find a way of getting away on their own by whatever transportation they might be able to obtain. Men from sixteen to sixty years of age, who had been exempt from military service for reasons of age, health, and indispensability, were generally required to remain to serve in the Volkssturm or Volk Storm, a form of late home defense guard that was organized in September 1944. During the summer of that year, many males, reaching down to fourteen-year-olds, had been recruited to dig defense trenches behind the front lines. I was only twelve, and thus escaped the duty of shoring up the defense of the German Reich. My father eluded the draft into the Volkssturm due to his physical limitation, as he had managed earlier to stay out of the regular army. My parents and I were very fortunate to remain together as a family throughout the war.

Late in January 1945 my father learned that the management of the estate on which we were staying was organizing an evacuation trek. The German estate owner, who earlier had sent his wife and two children to a town in eastern Pomerania about 170 miles west of Zuckau, agreed to include us in the short caravan of two horse-drawn wagons. The owner himself, I believe, was not allowed to leave the area, but he directed his estate manager to lead the trek. It carried, in addition to the manager, an elderly woman friend of the estate owner, my parents and me and, on a second wagon, a family of Ukrainians who had been working as farm laborers on the estate. I never learned whether this family had come to West Prussia of their own volition, trying to flee from the advancing Red Army or, more likely, had been deported for labor by the Germans a year or two before. From whatever possessions we had brought from Lithuania to Zuckau, we were able to take only a reduced portion on our next leg of flight.

Our trek toward the west set out on January 29, during a snowy night. During the first two days the horses had to pull the wagons through fairly deep snow and so our progress was quite slow. As long as it was possible, I chose to make the early stretches of the trip on my skis rather than ride in the cold canvass enclosed wagon. The

Ukrainians rode in an open wagon. Once we got farther westward the roads were less snowy and our trek made more normal progress. Much of the time we did not travel on the main highways because they were often congested with refugee treks and military vehicles, but used secondary roads. Early in the evening we usually found some kind of shelter with families in farmhouses, and on two occasions on large estates. Since food was still available on ration cards in towns or villages on the road, we had enough to eat while we were traveling. What made the trip uncomfortable were the cold temperatures, since they often fell well below freezing.

One of the most interesting stops that we made was in Varzin, about 75 miles from Zuckau, which, as we learned, had been one of Otto von Bismarck's estates. Here we even extended our overnight stay to half a day's rest. The manager of the Varzin estate and his wife were friendly and not only offered food and shelter but also, to my surprise, very revealing conversation. They were obviously disillusioned with the Nazis and probably had never supported Hitler. It was from them that I first heard that Jews had actually been systematically killed in gas chambers. I already knew from an earlier overheard conversation that Jews were being persecuted and many of them in Lithuania and elsewhere had been shot. As for German Jews, it was generally reported in private that they had been deported to ghettoes and labor camps in the "east" after 1941-43, but little became known about their actual fate except to small numbers of people in Germany. Even our hosts in Varzin were not aware of the monstrous magnitude of the Nazi terror and murder perpetrated against Jews and others in Eastern Europe which became widely known after the war. They were, to my mind, also remarkably naïve in anticipating what the imminent Soviet occupation might be like. The wife of the estate manager remarked that Russian soldiers would likely be humane and would respond in kind when received with hospitality. She obviously did not believe some of the horror

stories that Goebbels's propaganda spread about the behavior of Soviet troops when they first invaded German territory in East Prussia
in 1944. For once, Goebbels was not off the mark in his prediction
that widespread pillage, rape, murder, and deportation lay in store for
German civilians once they fell into Soviet hands. We never learned
what became of our friendly hosts. When the Russians conquered
Pomerania, they dealt often brutally with owners and managers of
estates. A few were shot outright, others quickly rounded up and
deported to labor camps in the region and later to the Soviet Union
under abysmal conditions.

We were on the road for over two weeks. After traveling about
170 miles we reached a town called Wangerin, less than 80 miles
from Stettin on the Oder River. Apparently the manager's instruction was to meet the estate owner's wife and her two children in
order to turn over some of the baggage that they had not been able
to take with them. They were already on a train that was to leave in
a day or so. After unloading the belongings of the estate family, the
manager and leader of the trek announced that he had decided to
head back to Zuckau. I think my parents did not have the presence
of mind at that point to find a way of continuing our flight into the
interior of Germany to escape from the advancing Red Army. True,
we would have gotten into areas of central Germany that suffered
regular Anglo-American bombing raids and thus would have faced
a greater risk of harm. Also, there was no definite destination that we
knew to move to, since all of our close relatives and friends lived in
eastern Germany. My father said we would not return to West Prussia but would find a place to stay in Pomerania.

He remembered the widowed Baltic German father and his
daughter with whom we had been staying on one of the overnight
stops and suggested that we be dropped off there. Their name von
Vietinghoff indicated that they had once been members of the Baltic
German nobility, but now lived under modest conditions in Germany,

having moved there after losing their property in Estonia or Latvia after World War I. What probably appealed to my father was to be in the company of someone who also came from the Baltic region. Most important to him was that we remained in an area of Germany that contained only Germans rather than returned to the Germanized West Prussia which had a mixed population of Germans and Poles. After a few days of trekking eastward we reached Vellin, a village less than 50 miles south of the Baltic coast. The retired Baltic German nobleman and his daughter, whom we had met less than two weeks before, took us in. Their house was spacious enough to afford us satisfactory temporary living quarters. It was mid-February and we settled in this temporary refuge after almost three weeks on the road, looking to the future with uncertainty and little hope.

For food, we could obtain many of the necessary provisions in the village but others we had to get from stores in a nearby town called Pollnow, about four miles away. A few days after landing in Vellin, I walked to Pollnow to buy a few groceries. The main streets were filled with refugee wagons that were taking a short rest. To my surprise, I recognized several of my cousins from Pilviškiai who were sitting on one of the carriages and also soon spotted my Aunt Olga Reinert. We exchanged some of the most recent family news since we had been out of touch for several months. When I suggested to her that she and the other relatives might want to take a few days of rest in the village where my parents were staying, she very quickly said no, adding that she and the relatives wanted to push on and get over the Oder River while there was still time. In retrospect, she was absolutely right not to wait. After the war we learned that they had reached the Oder only hours before a bombing raid severely damaged the bridge which they had crossed, causing heavy casualties among the treks that were behind them. By the end of March they had made it safely to northwestern Germany and reached an area of Germany that was taken by British troops.

While we were on the road, the front line to the east stabilized for a while and so did the long wedge of the Soviet front line that had been thrust toward the Oder at the end of January. Along the wedge the front line was between 70 and 80 miles to the south of us and remained at that distance until the last week in February when the Red Army, assisted by Polish divisions, started its offensive to conquer all of Pomerania. After staying in Vellin a little more than week, we were hearing the rumble of firing artillery, announcing the approach of the front line. For just a few days, fairly strong German resistance briefly slowed down the advance of the Soviet forces. We also observed overflights of Russian airplanes in Vellin. They did not attack the village but dropped a few bombs at some distance. Around February 21 Pollnow was the target of a minor bombing raid. A few days later some of us listened to one of the last radio speeches of the Nazi propaganda minister Joseph Goebbels, still proclaiming his confidence in a final German victory. It was in this incongruous setting with a small group of neighbors of our host father-daughter couple that I dared as a thirteen-year-old to laugh aloud at this blatant lie. The rest of the listeners did not show any emotion, as I recall. The Russian troops seized control of the area by first occupying the towns and leaving much of the countryside to be mopped up later. Soviet tanks and infantry occupied Pollnow already on February 27, after a short-lived strong defense of the town by a German infantry unit had enabled its civilians to evacuate to the countryside (Murawski 184, 387). Several days later, when Soviet troops were getting closer to Vellin some villagers fled from their homes and hid in nearby woods and ravines. My parents decided to remain in the village with the Baltic family and several neighbors nearby.

References

Blum, Arkadius, ed. *Unsere Familiengeschichte eingebettet in die Geschichte unseres Volkes und der Weltpolitik von 1731-1981.* Augsburg: J. Walch, 1983.

Duffy, Christopher. *Red Storm on the Reich: The Soviet March on Germany, 1945.* New York: Da Capo Press, 1991.

Murawski, Erich. *Die Eroberung Pommerns durch die Rote Armee.* Boppard am Rhein: Harald Boldt Verlag, 1961.

S I X

Under Soviet Occupation

Terrible Days and a Nightmare Year

Regular small arms fire and sporadic tank shots during the late afternoon and evening of March 3, 1945, announced that Soviet units were near Vellin. No one slept during the night as we sat fully clothed in the living room of our host family waiting what would come next. Suddenly, an hour before daybreak, there was a Russian shout "stoi" (stop) followed by a burst of a light automatic gun fire close to our house. Within a minute there was very loud pounding on the door of the house. The landlord and my dad opened the door and three very agitated soldiers pointed their submachine guns at them and then at the rest of us. They calmed down a bit when the Baltic nobleman and my dad addressed them in Russian. They wanted to know if there were any German soldiers in the house. Then, before leaving, they demanded our watches and rings. The reason for the Russian soldiers' initial extra excitement was most likely the next door neighbor's attempt to run to our house. When ordered to stop, he did not do so because he did not know any Russian He was shot dead and lay on the street, covered by snow, for a week before his widow and her two daughters were able to bury him. That family suffered not only the loss of their husband and father but the young adult daughters had to endure repeated rapes by soldiers in the days that followed.

At the first sight of daybreak we and other villagers were ordered out of our houses and driven to the large courtyard of the nearby estate. My mother had packed a small suitcase with some basic necessities and that was all we could salvage from the house at that time. For several hours men and older boys were separated from women and children, kept assembled in the courtyard, while the women and children were ordered to stay in a cow barn next to the courtyard. Since most men of the village were serving in the military and away from their families, there were only younger teenage boys and mostly men over sixty in our group. Different Russian soldiers and noncom officers examined identity papers of the men, sometimes asked brief questions, and usually demanded watches, rings, and sometimes pocketknives. Not many people still had watches and rings. I did not have a watch but my pocketknife found a new owner very quickly. Since my dad spoke Russian, at one point one of the lower ranked officers accused him of being a spy. Fortunately the interrogator did not persist in his suspicion any further when my father firmly denied the allegation and said he was only an ordinary civilian.

After all of us had been standing in the courtyard for a while, my dad said to one of the soldiers: "Why don't you line us up and shoot us and get it over with." His response was: "We don't shoot civilians." The check of identity papers seems to have been for the purpose of identifying the owner and manager of the estate, men connected with government and the Nazi party, and some local professionals like lawyers and pastors, in order to arrest them and to send them to labor camps. The local manager of the estate and the Lutheran pastor were among the first to be arrested and taken away. My father was careful to keep any papers on him which indicated his service as a pastor well hidden; some of them he later destroyed. After several hours the men and older boys were allowed to join the women and children in the cow barn. Here we stayed through the night until the next day. During the night younger women had the worst of it, for they could not run away or hide when soldiers came again and again to pick one or several of them for what they had been told they could now do with impunity to German women: raping, beating, or even shooting them. In other situations the age of women did not matter to the violators, whether intoxicated or not, they violently abused very young as well as very old women.

As the rest of Soviet-conquered Germany, Vellin became the site of mass rape by Russian soldiers, who were given free reign (Stalin condoned if not encouraged such behavior); hate propaganda incited them to take their revenge on German civilians and especially German women for weeks and months to come, and there was also some shooting of German civilians. The widespread barbarism of plunder, rape, murder, and deportation that German forces had inflicted on the native population of Soviet Russia during their invasion and occupation of Soviet lands was now being repaid. But it was not only German women who were victims of widespread rape. Earlier when Soviet troops invaded new countries many women in Poland, the Baltic States, Rumania, Hungary, and even in Yugoslavia (which under Tito was a Soviet ally) had endured a similar fate.

During the next day many of us in the cow barn were directed to move to the mansion of the estate, where we were assigned rooms and kept for several days before being released for return to the village. Once we got back to the village houses, people noticed that some of their friends or acquaintances were missing. In several instances, not in Vellin, but in neighboring communities families had committed suicide shortly before the Soviet troops arrived. A few of the missing no doubt were still hiding in woods nearby, but others seemed to have disappeared. Those that did not return in the weeks and months that followed were most likely among the deportees transported to Soviet Russia to be used there as forced labor. It was usually men and women between 18 and 45 years of age who were selected for deportation because they were deemed to be fit for hard labor. As mentioned earlier, there were not many men in the able-bodied age range left and so sometimes even boys younger than eighteen ended up among the deportees. The major deportation waves from our region occurred in March and April. It did not matter to the soldiers who had been ordered to round up a certain number of men and women for deportation whether fathers or mothers were separated from their children or their families. I remember witnessing the sad scene of a young mother being torn from her recently born baby. As we learned years later, about half a million German civilians were forcefully shipped to the interior of the Soviet Union in unheated freight cars, often with little or no food, and, after weeks of travel, distributed for forced labor in western Russia, the Ural region, and Siberia. Almost half of them never saw Germany again. They succumbed to the harsh working conditions, lack of adequate food (even many of the Soviet civilians at that time endured food shortages), poor hygienic conditions, and disease. Some lucky ones were released within a year and allowed to return to Germany if they became ill and could no longer work; but most of the others were kept there for two, three, and sometimes more years.

When we returned to the house where we had stayed with the Baltic father-daughter couple, we found it in shambles. It had been pillaged and vandalized, even used as a privy. A few of our possessions that had not been looted by the soldiers were strewn all over; a small radio which we had carried with us was totally demolished. Presumably, the Russians feared that radio sets might be used by Germans for "intelligence" purposes. My parents decided not to remain in that house, since it was too close to the main road through the village and therefore more exposed to unfriendly Russian visitors. We moved in with a local farmer family, consisting of a mother and two young teenage sons, in the center of Vellin. My dad right away took on the job of looking after a local bread oven, which several of the village families used for baking their bread. That way we were assured of access to regular bread since he was "paid" in loaves of bread from time to time. Together with my dad I helped caring for the several cows on the small farm of our host family; we cleaned the cow barn every morning and fed the animals. There were still some chickens left on the farm which occasionally produced a few eggs. Our basic food necessities were thus met since the family we stayed with shared whatever else they could still glean from their farm.

We were living, however, in constant uncertainty if not fear, not knowing what may happen next. There were always Russian soldiers passing through, looking for food and live chickens, or demanding household goods, clothes, and blankets. A few of them showed their lack of familiarity with common Western household items. I remember one asking what a fork is used for. Later on we heard stories of soldiers mistaking toilet bowls (in houses that had indoor plumbing) for washing basins. What astounded many soldiers was that not only farmers but also farm workers in our community lived in houses, often made of brick, and equipped with what we regarded as just very basic furnishings. A few asked, "Why did Hitler come to Russia if he had all that in Germany?" On several occasions soldiers and officers stayed overnight. Since my dad could communicate with them, it was easier to know what the "visitors" were after. When addressed in their own language, their behavior would quite often become more civil. It was more difficult when a group of soldiers came swarming over the farmyard and could not be dealt with on an individual basis. After looking around for a while, occasionally going through the house, they would leave taking something or other along. Once several soldiers came into the farmyard and became annoyed by the barking of the farm dog. One of them simply shot him.

For the most part, we were fortunately spared major violent harassment during these weeks. However we were cut off from reliable news about the outside world. There were no newspapers, let alone radio transmissions even if someone had secretly managed to save a workable set. All we heard was what was related by word of mouth about what was happening in the region and in the country, and very little of that was credible. Here and there my dad would get some comments about current events from soldiers, but they did not provide a larger picture except that the war was continuing. We soon experienced how conditions of news deprivation can breed rumor mongering with fantastic stories based on wishful thinking. In the first two or three weeks of the occupation, we heard several "reports" that German soldiers had been sighted in some not too distant locations, and that our liberation was near. Some people even suggested that it would be best to hide out in the woods while waiting to be rescued. After several weeks had gone by and liberation by German troops was no longer plausible, other versions of "liberation" hope spread: American troops had been seen in a nearby region and we could expect to have the Soviet occupation replaced by the American. Such stories might have had merit in central Germany where Soviet and Western Allied troops shifted from some areas in accordance with the drawn borders of occupation zones; but they made no sense in an area like Pomerania far away from the British and American occupation zones. We heard nothing of the Allied agreements on the establishment of occupation zones. After five or more weeks with more problems and rumor mongering lost its appeal as a glimmer of hope.

One day in the latter part of April Russian soldiers appeared in Vellin to assemble a railroad dismantling crew. Even though I was only thirteen years old, I was drafted for this work together with a fair number of men and women from the village. We were marched several miles to a nearby community to start removing the tracks of a railroad branch line.

During the first full day of work, a track that was being flipped over on the ground fell on my right big toe. Fortunately I wore fairly heavy shoes so that even though the injury was painful, it did not cause permanent damage to my foot. After hobbling around for half a day, another boy and I decided that we would try to wander away from the work site and return to the village where our families were staying. Since there were not many guards around, the escape was fairly easy. In the evening the headcount in the room that we had been staying in for the night at the work site revealed our absence. And within a day a soldier came looking for replacements in our village. He recruited the oldest boy, who was two years older than I, from the farmer family with whom my parents had found shelter. Naturally, the native family was unhappy now to see one of their own taken away.

Only four or five days after I had returned to my anxious parents, Russian soldiers staged another roundup for a work crew, this time of village women. They were to drive most of the village cattle to a central point near a railroad station less than ten miles away for later shipment to the Soviet Union. As in the case of the railroad track dismantling, this was another attempt of the Soviets to take whatever could be pillaged from the area before the Poles came to occupy it. We eventually learned that all of Pomerania was to be turned over to the Poles. My mother was among those selected to go with the cattle that was being taken away. At that point, my father wisely decided that we all would go with the trek in order not be separated as a family. We joined the cattle trek with whatever few personal possessions we could take with us, never to return to Vellin. The Baltic nobleman made the same decision to go with his daughter when she was taken along. We all ended up in Silberhof, a small community with a large estate about ten miles from Vellin, where we stayed over three weeks. Large herds of cattle were amassed there outdoors which needed to be regularly milked and fed. The house we were assigned to stay in also had some Lithuanians and French prisoners of war, who were hoping to be repatriated soon. The Baltic nobleman readily conversed with the Frenchmen, since he spoke French as fluently as he did Russian. My parents communicated with several of the Lithuanians.

Whether many of the cattle ever ended up in Russia is doubtful. Pomeranian farm animals were used to being kept well sheltered during the cold months rather than left to fend for themselves under the elements. Even in April it was still too early to leave cattle in the open day and night. By concentrating large herds of them in one locale, the risk of disease was magnified. Not surprisingly, quite a few cattle soon caught some cow disease or other, including the dreaded hoof and mouth disease. We did not stay long enough in Silberhof to find out how many of the cattle survived there. Similarly, farm machinery was collected and concentrated near railroad junctions to be shipped to the Soviet Union. But exposed to snow and rain, much of the machinery began to rust and became less useful.

After a few weeks my mother found tending the cattle and also working in the community kitchen too strenuous, and my father managed to get her excused by volunteering to take her place. He however was not assigned to look after cows but was quickly engaged by the Russian commandant and soldiers as translator. As for myself, I stayed out of sight as much as possible in order to avoid being drafted for employment. One day in Silberhof my father learned from several Russian soldiers that the war had finally ended, but they provided no further details and so we heard nothing about how Germany and Germans were going to be treated in the war's aftermath.

About the third week of May many of us were ordered to move to a nearby village called Hanshagen, where the Russians decided to establish a temporary collective farm. We found housing in a two-story multi-dwelling farm worker building, which also had several stables nearby where farm workers kept their own animals. Some of the former farm workers were still there but many of us were newcomers. Hanshagen was located about 17 miles south of the town of Schlawe, today Slawno, less than twenty or so miles from the Baltic Sea. The village community consisted largely of an estate and had employed thirty or forty farm laborers during German times.

My father was kept busy working during the day as translator and before long was also assigned the record keeping of the newly formed "collective farm," which in reality was a modified version of the earlier German estate administration. He had to keep daily records of how many hours farm workers spent on the job and how much they earned in Russian rubles and kopecks. The recorded compensation was very small and while he was working there not even one kopeck was ever paid to anyone who was employed on this collective farm. Our own food situation was tolerable, since we could still get potatoes from the previous year's crop on the estate, flour for bread, and some vegetables. Essential for our nutritional sustenance was a cow that my dad arranged to obtain from the Soviet commandant, which was of course one of the German animals that were left on the estate. It was a fairly young milk cow that had had a bout with the hoof and mouth disease which left it limping. But important for us, it produced a moderate amount of milk every day. My mother turned some of the milk into cheese and also butter. I became a cowherd, taking care of the feeding and pasturing of the complacent bovine, and also learned to milk it, though perhaps not very efficiently. . There was a bit of concern for a while when the palm of my left hand swelled up one day with considerable pain and continued to enlarge for several days. The inflammation was probably due to a pock infection contracted from our cow. When the large boil seemed to be "ripe" my father lanced it with his razor, relieving the discomfort very quickly. After several weeks I was again milking our cow. My bout with this infection was just a reminder of how vulnerable we all were to the vagaries of disease apart from daily concerns of survival.

Life during these months in Hanshagen continued to be unpredictable but we did not experience as much harassment from Russian soldiers as we had in Vellin. From time to time there were changes in local commandants and the small troop of soldiers who occupied the village. Violent incidents happened mostly when some of the local soldiers became intoxicated and unpredictable and looked for women to abuse. We noticed that several of the commandants had acquired German girl friends that kept them generally satisfied. But incidents of rape and plundering continued to be reported with distressing frequency. There was one refugee physician in the village, but he could not provide real help when women came to him with venereal disease complaints and other medical problems, since he had very little by way of medicines and he did not stay very long in the community. We did not hear of penicillin, the treatment for venereal and other infections, until we moved to the American zone one year later. Several women who had become pregnant as a result of rapes tried to induce abortions. Those who did not try to abort gave birth to "Russian" babies.

I came to know several neighbor children my age or younger, whose mothers had been deported. Relatives looked after the children, and one father, who due to a physical disability had escaped the German military draft during the war and Soviet deportation later. These children missed their mothers badly and around Christmas time 1945 I saw them wandering up the hilly main road that went by our house, hoping that they might see their mothers returning home at last.

I felt very fortunate that I was still with my parents. By staying out of sight as much as possible I avoided being recruited for work on the collective farm. Besides looking after our cow, usually with a neighborhood dog that I had befriended, I spent quite a bit of time reading adventure story books which I discovered in the house where we were staying. It was a lucky accident for me to run across books that were usually devoured by boys my age: Daniel Defoe's *Robinson Crusoe* and several of Karl May's fascinating adventure tales, dealing with American Indians and natives in other parts of the world. Karl May never traveled much outside of Germany and had even spent some time in jail, but he had a marvelous imagination creating adventure stories that have captivated young teenage German boys for generations. Here and there I also read a few adult novels. All of this reading was a welcome escape from the uncertainties of life around me. My father started teaching me some Russian, but at that time I made little progress in that difficult language. Once we escaped from the Soviet occupation I forgot whatever I had learned and did not return to Russian language study until many years later in my life.

Both of my parents outwardly tried to take life as it came, day by day. Looking to the future, they wondered if there would be enough food left in our area since crops in the spring and fall of 1945 had not been planted as usual. Then, what was to become of the Germans under Soviet and Polish administration? They continued to be treated as outlaws whom anyone could harm with impunity.

We did not learn of the Allied decisions made about the future of Germany at various high level conferences by Franklin Roosevelt, Winston Churchill, and Joseph Stalin between 1943 and 1945 until we escaped from the Soviet-occupied part of Germany in 1946. All we heard in Pomerania was that most of the province had been conquered by the Red Army and a few areas by Polish troops. During the months while we were there some places were vacated by the Soviets and Poles were taking them over. In several of the Polish-occupied areas Germans were being forced out immediately and pushed towards the regions west of the Oder River. The Soviet military appeared to be confused as to what to do with the masses of German and non-German civilians under their control. Several soldiers told us everyone should go back to his home or homeland. This meant Russian and Ukrainian civilians were to return to the Soviet Union, Lithuanians and other Balts to their respective homelands, the French prisoners of war to France, and presumably Germans to the regions from which they originally came. It was not clear whether East Prussians and West Prussians should do the same. Since my dad's passport indicated Lithuania as the land of origin, we feared that this could mean we might be shipped back there.

One of the local Soviet commandants told my dad that things were rather "chaotic here," and therefore he should come to the Soviet Union with the Russians. On the other hand, some friendly Russian civilians, who had no choice but to return to their homeland, warned my dad and urged him to move westward to the interior of Germany whenever he saw a chance to do so. Certainly my dad had no illusions about conditions in the Soviet interior, since he had been forced to live in Russia and the Ukraine during World War I and was not able to return to Lithuania until 1921, after the Bolshevik Revolution and the bitter Civil War. Facing daily the uncertain and abnormal local living conditions, hearing again and again from villagers of continuing violence, worrying that there might be more deportations of German civilians, my dad concluded there was no normal life possible for Germans under the Soviet and Polish regimes. In the last few months before our escape from Pomerania, he said: "I am going to lose my mind if I stay here much longer." We decided to move westward from Hanshagen at the earliest opportunity, even if this meant undertaking travel during the cold winter months rather than waiting until the spring. The only question was how this could be arranged.

Our Last Flight

We heard that trains were running from time to time from Schlawe (now Slavno), a town about 17 miles north of us, to Stettin (now Szczecin) on the Oder River but we considered public transportation risky. My dad was the only Russian-speaking German in the community left after the Baltic nobleman and his daughter returned to their home village in the previous summer. He was in daily contact with the local Russian commandant and other Russians who needed him for various translation services, and would have missed

him quickly if he did not show up for work. It was therefore necessary to arrange our departure quietly and in secret and to avoid using public transportation. The opportunity came when my dad heard
that two other families in Hanshagen were also planning an early
escape. The heads of these families were skilled in repairing machinery, vehicles, radios, and appliances and therefore indispensable
to the local Russian occupiers. Through their work they had met
several Poles who occupied a community about 12 miles from Hanshagen. Some of these Poles were members of the Polish militia,
which was instrumental in setting up the civilian administration of
the Polish government.

At this time there were National Poles and Communist Poles.
The former recognized the Polish exile government in London as
the legitimate government of Poland, whereas the latter followed
the Communist Lublin government that had been instituted under
Stalin and preempted the authority of the Polish National government in exile. Both Polish factions were hostile toward Germans
but National Poles were at times more humane toward Germans,
who otherwise were treated as outlaws by Poles and Russians
alike. Many Polish military units and militia contingents had been
established under both the National and Communist governments
and had strong ideological differences. In the negotiations of the
heads of the two German families with their National Polish acquaintances, they agreed to provide transportation to Berlin for
three German families for a price. The Poles wanted the three German cows that we three families had acquired and also some jewelry that one of the families had managed to save from all the earlier pillage. What further motivated the National Poles was their
chance "to get back" at our local Russians, several of whom had
beaten up two of the Polish militiamen several weeks earlier in
Hanshagen. The arrangements were set for our pickup at a designated small forest, less than half a mile away from our village

at midnight on February 8, 1946. We had less than a week to get ready for our getaway.

One major challenge was to keep our plan secret from all the villagers. This was not always possible, though when asked we all strongly denied that anything was being contemplated by us at the time. The other two families lived in the center of the village and so their preparations aroused some suspicion of neighbors, but fortunately no one blabbered to the Russians. My father mentioned our plan only to a next door neighbor one day before our departure because he was to help us get our cow quietly out of the shed without arousing any suspicion among our other neighbors. In return we promised to take news of his and his children's survival to his relatives in Berlin. This neighbor's wife had been deported and he had not had any news of her. We also needed a document from a Polish administrative office in Schlawe to legitimate our travel.

For this purpose, very early on February 5, which happened to be my fourteenth birthday, two women representing the other two families and I hiked seventeen miles to Schlawe. The other adults did not dare leave the village for fear of arousing unnecessary suspicion. The women and I were successful in getting to the appropriate office on time to each get a simple document on thin paper, stating in Polish that the named persons of our respective families were being expelled from the region. I myself did not really know what was written on the parchment paper until my dad, with the help of his Russian, was able to give an approximate translation. The document ensured our legitimate travel to Berlin and then through the Soviet-occupied zone to Bavaria, where some of our relatives lived under American occupation.

Since we were too tired to start our return hike and it would have been inadvisable to wander about at night, we sought shelter for the night. After several futile inquiries at German homes we were lucky to be taken in by a Polish family. The father, an older man, examined us closely but concluded from our newly acquired documents that we could be trusted. He spoke enough broken German so that we could communicate. It turned out to be an interesting evening conversation. This man and his family had come from the area of prewar Poland that had been annexed by the Soviet Union. Most of the Polish population was being transferred from there to the regions of eastern Germany which were now being vacated by the expulsion of Germans. These Polish refugees were being placed in formerly German homes, which generally still had German furniture and household goods because their owners were not allowed to take along more than hand baggage. This Polish man obviously knew what refugee life was like and showed some human compassion.

The next day we returned without incident to Hanshagen and could go about firming up our escape preparations. For weeks my mother had cut up bread into small pieces and then dried them to take along on our risky journey westward. We could not expect to find food just wherever we ended up. My parents also managed to get some Polish currency by trading some butter. We knew that baggage could easily be searched for whatever Russians or Poles wanted from Germans or even taken away altogether. Reports of people having clothes stolen from their backs and shoes from their feet were distressingly common. My mother had the imaginative idea that we could make our good clothes look shabby by stitching patches on them and pouring candle wax on our coats, jackets, her dresses, and skirts, and also on our shoes. Since it was winter we expected to wear several layers of outer clothes without any discomfort; and this also lightened the load of the baggage that we carried.

Our dwelling was on the outskirts of Hanshagen and conveniently located by the road that we planned to use for the getaway. Two nights before our flight the men of the other families brought most of their luggage to our place so that it could later be moved without attracting notice. It was stowed against the wall of one of our backrooms and covered with canvas. The next day we had some anxious moments when one of the local Russian soldiers came to our place and started looking at all the walls for picture frames. Fortunately he was so preoccupied searching for what he wanted that he never looked down to examine what might be under the cover of the stored luggage. I think he left our house without actually finding the kind of frame that suited him.

In the evening of February 8, fully packed and ready to depart, there was however one thing left to do, namely, to take care of the dog that had been my companion for most of our stay in Hanshagen. It was an older animal and had been left in the neighborhood so I adopted it. I felt bad just to leave the dog to an uncertain fate and so my dad found a way to mercifully end its life. Even though I felt sad to lose it, I was also relieved that it would not have to fend for itself, perhaps never finding anyone to take care of it. My dad probably had also considered the possibility that the dog might bark when our cow was led out of the shed in the middle of the night. This no doubt would have waked the neighbors who did not know of our plans.

The Poles who agreed to help us in our escape kept their word and waited for us at the designated small wood slightly off the main road and not far from the outskirts of the village around midnight. They came with two wagons, one covered, the other open, to pick up all the three families, their baggage and the three cows. I noticed when we reached our Polish helpers, several were armed and standing behind trees with their guns at the ready. One family in our group included the parents, several children, an elderly grandmother, and a brother who was paralyzed. The brother needed much help to move about. The other family consisted of two parents and several children. After our baggage was loaded onto the wagons, the adults who could not easily walk and the children were put on the covered wagon. The cows were tied to the open wagon, and then the trek got underway. All the able-bodied adults walked beside or behind the trek. One worry was that the recent snowfall left our tracks on the road. Since there had been little traffic on the road, it would not have been difficult to follow our tracks if someone had really wanted to pursue our escape party.

We traveled for several hours to reach the community where the Poles that were helping us in our getaway were stationed at that time. To our surprise we met several parties of Russians in carriages and in wagons on the road moving in the opposite direction. But they seemed to take no notice of us, strange as our trek might have appeared to be. In one instance, my dad recognized one of the Russians from a neighboring community, who occasionally stopped by in Hanshagen. My dad hoped that the Russian had not recognized him. We were encountering Russian civilians traveling to the next major town to vote in the first postwar election, which the Stalin regime was holding on February 9 throughout the Soviet Union and in Soviet-occupied areas of Europe. Soviet soldiers and nationals were expected to participate in this event and many had to start very early in the morning to reach their voting place. I imagine that the attention of the Russians in Hanshagen was also distracted by this activity, and thus it probably took them longer than it would have otherwise to discover that most of their German "intelligentsia" were no longer available to serve them.

As we continued our journey, for my parents, trudging along on the snowy road became difficult and especially my mother was falling farther and farther behind the trek. Fortunately, for the last stretch of the trip she was allowed to ride on the open wagon. Once we branched off on a side road that was to take us to our destination, a Pole appeared with a small wagon and began to drag some straw over the tracks that were left behind us on the road. In the early morning we reached Zitzmin, the village occupied by the Poles who were helping us. We stayed there until February 12. It was a relief to have some rest before we embarked on the next stage of our trip.

In the evening of the day for our departure we were told to load our baggage on a mid-sized truck that was to take us to Berlin, which we still believed was our next destination. Very soon it became obvious there were nineteen or twenty adults and children so not all the baggage would fit on this vehicle. We had no choice but to leave our bedding and some other possessions behind, including the ice skates that I treasured as a memento of my late cousin Alfons Schulz. The ride started around eight o'clock in the evening and was the worst truck ride of my life. We all were crammed close together sitting or reclining on the baggage pieces, often in uncomfortable positions. But at least we were hopefully getting farther and farther away from places that had no future for us. The truck was covered and the Polish party, a man driver and a woman, hoped to get through the road checkpoints without having to show what they were transporting. On several occasions they knocked on the back of the cabin to warn us to keep noise, especially crying children, down or subdued in order not to arouse suspicion when we approached road checks. We made no stops until we got to Scheune near Stettin, which served as a border crossing point from the Soviet and Polish occupied Pomerania to the Soviet occupation zone of Germany west of the Oder River. We had traveled about 130 miles to reach the railroad station of Scheune. It was early in the morning and still dark. I don't know if anyone of our escape party knew that our truck ride would end there rather than in Berlin. By dropping us off at a train station and at a time when a train was expected to leave for Berlin soon must have appeared to the Poles who brought as there as sufficient to fulfill the terms of the original agreement, i.e. "to provide transportation to Berlin."

When we entered the railroad station hall, we found a crowd of excited German passengers waiting. The reason for the excitement was, as several of them quickly told us, that only ten minutes before our arrival they had been raided by a Polish band who had robbed them of many of their possessions. We certainly had heard many stories of such incidents before. Some time after daybreak a passenger train pulled into the station and all of us were allowed to board it, hoping that we finally were on our way to Berlin. When the train started out several hours later, some of us noticed that Russian soldiers were jumping on the train cars. The reason for their taking the train ride became obvious quite quickly. Claiming that they needed some clothes for their wounded comrades, they proceeded to take coats, jackets, and other clothing items from the German men. Not many passengers escaped their unwelcome attention. They even forced the paralyzed man of our party to give up his suit jacket. My dad had decided that he would no longer indicate that he spoke Russian in order not to risk being recruited as a translator or interpreter. For some reason the soldiers did not demand anything from him or me. Later my dad reported that he overheard one of the soldiers saying to another: "These people," meaning my parents and me, "are Poles, and we will not touch them." Had our "shabby" looking disguised clothes saved us from the attention of the Russian soldiers?

After several hours of fairly slow travel the train stopped in Angermünde, a town half way between Stettin and Berlin. We had covered a distance of about 50 miles. Much to our unhappy surprise we were told that this was as far as the train could travel, for a flood had washed out a railroad bridge ahead and disrupted all rail travel to Berlin. There was no indication how long the disruption would last. We were all directed to find shelter in the local refugee camp. We had to walk less than a mile to get there with our baggage. The other two families had a more difficult time than we since one of the men had practically to carry his paralyzed brother, and his mother was also not able to walk very easily. The camp was located in a public building and had several large rooms. It was a dismal sight. There were many people there. Some looked so emaciated as if almost at death's door (and a few would actually die every day or night); others appeared to be ill, only a few were still able-bodied. We stayed there for the night, sleeping on the bare floor. Some of the dried bread that we were carrying served as our meal for the day after we had dunked it in heated water.

The next morning my parents decided to find out whether there was any kind of transportation available to get to Berlin. I stayed at the camp guarding our baggage. By asking around they met a family who lived in town and had several relatives staying with them who were planning to travel to Berlin the next morning. These people knew that persons wanting to travel to Berlin had a good chance of catching a ride on trucks by lining up in the early morning at a junction of the main road of the city. This was welcome news and my parents asked these new acquaintances to permit us to store some of our baggage at their house overnight. We lost track of the other two families who had fled with us from Pomerania.

After my parents had firmed up a promising opportunity to leave Angermünde, it was my turn to look around in the town. It was encouraging to be in an area under German administration and whose population was German, except for the Russian military. Conditions seemed to be more orderly here than in Pomerania but, as I discovered, not without certain risks. When I was on my way back to the camp after a brief look around town, I noticed that less than a short block away a Soviet soldier was forcing some people on the street to join a group that he was recruiting for some work assignment. I managed to duck into a doorway of a backyard and observed what was happening on the street without being seen. After a while the street seemed to be safe again, and I quickly returned to the camp, where my parents and I spent the second and last night in Angermünde.

Very early the next morning we retrieved our stored baggage and assembled at the junction from where we were to hitchhike to Berlin. We became better acquainted with the two women, also on their way to Berlin, whom my parents had met the day before; they were actually returning to their family in Berlin after a visit in An-germünde. Before long an open truck stopped and allowed us to get into the back. There were already a few persons there and later even some Russian soldiers or noncom officers joined us. They tried to engage my dad in conversation but he did not let on that he under-stood their language, and so it became a truncated exchange. When we entered the city of Berlin, we saw more and more ruins and badly damaged buildings as we approached the center of the city, marking the widespread destruction of the German capital. The small party of our new acquaintances from Angermünde asked to be dropped off at Alexanderplatz, the main square in the city center, for their family lived within walking distance of that landmark of Berlin. Not having any definite contacts yet that we might turn to in the city, my dad asked if we could leave our baggage temporarily at their family's home. Having done so we took to the streets.

My dad remembered that the Methodist Church had a hospital in the city, and he hoped that if it had survived the war we might find temporary shelter there. While we were walking along on Unter den Linden, the main street of the capital, my parents spotted two deaconesses in white caps. My father stopped them and asked if they knew of a Methodist hospital in Berlin. These deaconesses were not Methodists, but they knew the name of the Methodist hospital, its location, and what streetcar to take to get there. They also mentioned that the hospital was located in the American sector of Berlin. The Alexanderplatz area was part of the Soviet sector but in 1946 it was still easy to cross sector borders in Berlin. However we were soon advised to stay out of the Soviet sector as much as possible, since the Soviet military carried out identity checks from time to time. We did not have any local identity papers and so we could have run into major difficulties if stopped. But being in a Soviet controlled area had become loathsome to us, and the Western sectors appeared to provide a bit of freedom and more security at last.

One lasting memory from that streetcar ride through the center of the city on our way to the Methodist hospital in Berlin-Steglitz was seeing not a single building intact for at least a mile or two. The street had been cleared of the rubble but both sides of the street were lined by yawning structures and ruins. Not all parts of Berlin had been so severely damaged, but most of the center of the city was left in a sea of ruins from years of Allied bombing and the fierce fighting of the final Battle of Berlin in April 1945.

At the hospital, my dad asked to see the director. To his pleasant surprise he knew him personally because both had been fellow students at the Frankfurt Methodist Theological Seminary in the early twenties. The director assured us that the hospital had provided temporary shelter for others and would do the same for us. This was naturally a great relief, for it would give us time to determine where to locate once we left Berlin. Certainly we were overdue for some rest and, most importantly, we were grateful to be in a relatively safe environment after almost a year of feeling like hunted hares. We had no ration cards but we were invited to participate in the community meals of the deaconess staff. Meals were well prepared but also reflected the rationing of food in the city. At mealtime it was announced how much everyone could have: one or two slices of bread for breakfast or at supper time, a small portion of butter or jam, a slice of cheese, occasionally one egg; never more than one potato for dinner, a small portion of meat, etc. Even though no one rose hungry from the table, probably everyone could have easily eaten more. Nevertheless the meals were adequate to maintain one's strength and health.

Since we had been out of contact with all of our relatives for a year and a half and did not know where they were staying, or even if they had survived, my parents wondered how we might be able to locate them. They remembered that Oscar Schaudinat, Aunt Ottilie's brother (the wife of my dad's brother Karl) had moved to Berlin after we returned to Lithuania in 1942. He was married to a

Russian wife and so was his eldest son Emmanuel, and they were therefore not granted German citizenship. We found their address in the Berlin address directory. My parents were advised to send them a telegram rather than trying to visit them, since their address was in the Soviet sector. We soon learned that the Schaudinats had moved from their original residence in Berlin to the American sector, and our telegram was forwarded to their new address. Two days later Oscar Schaudinat visited us and we could rejoice in the first news of some of our relatives.

He told us that Uncle Karl Blum with his wife Ottilie and Aunt Alma Schulz together with Uncle Karl's oldest son Erwin and daughter Alida had managed to resettle in a village in Bavaria, which was in the American occupation zone. A cousin of my dad's had settled in nearby Bad Kissingen together with his family and grown children. During our stay in Berlin my mother also located an old friend of hers, originally from Tilsit, who was living in the Soviet sector of Berlin. She came by for a visit at the hospital and offered good advice about what to do and not to do in the city. In addition, we called on the Methodist Bishop of Germany, Dr. F. Melle, who also resided in a Western Allied sector of the city. He was very much interested in hearing about the conditions in Pomerania and the fate of Germans there. He had just been visited by John Mott, a prominent American churchman and YMCA leader, and regretted that he could not immediately share some of our accounts with his American visitor.

Even though Berlin for us was a breath of fresh air and a ray of hope for an eventual more orderly and normal life, the image of the city in the winter of 1946 presented a depressing sight. Public transportation, most services, and mail had been restored. Streets had been cleared of the rubble to allow traffic to pass through, but there had been little reconstruction of the vast areas of badly damaged and destroyed buildings. Only a few structures, which needed limited repair, were in full use. A chilling sight was the ropes left hanging from some of the lamp and telephone posts, usually with a sign indicating that a soldier, an officer, even a Hitler youth had been hanged here for desertion or treason by the military police or SS. Such public executions on the spot were often carried out toward the end of the war not only in Berlin but also throughout Germany to deter troops from deserting. The city population suffered from food shortages and, during the winter, from fuel shortages as well. Many of the trees that lined the streets and trees in parks were being cut down to be used for firewood. Sightseeing in Berlin was out of the question for us at that time. The most sightseeing that I did was to travel on a city train from one station to the end of the line and back, avoiding stretches that passed through the Soviet sector. On our brief visit to the Schaudinats' home in Berlin-Zehlendorf I was able to borrow one of their bikes to take a short ride along the shore of one of the nearby lakes on a sunny Sunday afternoon.

The city was carved up into Allied sectors which paralleled the division of Germany into military zones of occupation. Already in July 1941, only one month after Hitler's invasion of Russia, the Soviets proposed the dismemberment of Germany after the war and found support from the British and Americans in 1942. The proposal to dismember Germany and to subject Germans to harsh treatment persisted until early 1945, supported by Joseph Stalin and Franklin Roosevelt, but opposed by Winston Churchill after late 1944 and the American State and Defense Departments. The latter considered the impoverishment of Germany an enormous hindrance to the rebuilding of a prosperous Europe. What prevailed was the plan that was endorsed by the Big Three Roosevelt, Stalin, and Churchill at Teheran in 1943: the division of Germany into military occupation zones. The boundaries of these zones for Germany and the sectors for Berlin were not finalized until the Yalta Conference convened in early 1945. Several months later the French were included among the occupiers of Germany and Berlin.

Another idea, as early as 1943, the prospect of separating Germany east of the Oder River and ceding most of that area to Poland came under discussion as a way of compensating Poland for the loss of eastern Poland, which Stalin had already seized under the Nazi-Soviet Pact of 1939 and annexed during the advance of the Red Army into Germany. Stalin also added northern East Prussia to his domain in early 1945. The Polish problem was not settled until the Yalta Conference in February 1945 and the Potsdam Conference in July 1945, when Poland was given formal control of the German territories east of the Oder and Neisse rivers and the southern section of East Prussia.

Stalin also quite early insisted that Germany must pay reparations in the form of goods and labor to help restore the devastated areas of Soviet Russia. The Soviets and the Western Allies did not reach a formal agreement on reparations in 1945 but accepted, as a basis for discussion, Stalin's figure of $20 billion consisting of capital goods, industrial and agricultural production, and human labor. Of this total Russia claimed $10 billion. These Soviet claims became the justification for taking from the Soviet-controlled areas of Germany whatever was deemed useful to Russia and deporting half a million German civilians for forced labor in Soviet mines, factories, quarries, on construction projects, under generally inhumane conditions. (The deportation of German civilians was in addition to the almost three and half million German prisoners of war that ended up in Soviet hands.) The condition of the German civilian deportees and prisoners of war was worsened in the immediate years after the war by shortages of food throughout the Soviet Union, which also affected the native population.

The administration of Berlin entailed a shared arrangement under the Allied Control Council of the four occupying powers: U.S., Britain, Soviet Union, and France. Originally only the first three named allies were to share in the occupation of the German capital, but upon Winston Churchill's insistence the French were also assigned a sector of the city (and an occupation zone in Germany) at the Yalta Conference. In April and early May 1945 Berlin was conquered by the Red Army. However the Western Allies were only allowed to occupy their sectors in July, after the Americans had begun to withdraw from Saxony and Thuringia, which they had conquered but which, under Allied agreement, were to become part of the Soviet occupied domain.

When we reached Berlin in February 1945 we learned only some very general terms of the Allied agreements. They appeared to confirm what we had observed under Soviet and Polish occupation in Pomerania. My father felt very strongly that he did not want to stay in any Soviet-occupied territory but would shift to a part of Germany that was under American control. Berlin had Western enclaves but was surrounded by the Soviet occupation zone. My dad's colleague at the hospital suggested that he could find a Methodist congregation to serve as pastor in the Soviet zone, since there were vacancies. However my dad rejected that prospect and indicated that our much preferred option was to go to Bavaria to be closer to our relatives. Our stay in Berlin lasted six weeks, longer than we had anticipated, due to a painful large boil that my dad developed on his neck, requiring a physician's intervention. Soon we were ready to leave our temporary haven at the Methodist hospital. It was with some trepidation, however, that we anticipated traveling through the Soviet occupation zone to reach Bavaria.

Trains were operating fairly frequently on the main lines of Soviet-occupied Germany, but traveling on them was more difficult than one might imagine. They were always very crowded and it became risky to board trains at railroad stations because of the rush and often ruthless shoving of large crowds of anxious passengers. It was easy to fall and get trampled by them. On warmer days passengers even traveled on the roofs of train cars and on the sides. On cold days this was very dangerous. In the morning of March 19, we managed to get on a train with much difficulty that departed from Berlin-Wannsee and took us as far as Dessau, Saxony, where we had to wait until the next morning for a connecting train to Erfurt in Thuringia. Here we changed trains again to reach Eisenach, where we hoped to cross from the Soviet occupation zone to the American. We arrived there during the very early morning of March 21, and lined up at 5 o'clock at the Soviet border processing center together with hundreds of others. The Polish document that certified our expulsion from Pomerania, which I had obtained in Schlawe shortly before our escape from Hanshagen, and a definite address that we could indicate as our destination in Bavaria were sufficient to convince the German border officials and their Soviet supervisor to allow us to travel from the Soviet occupation zone to the American. My dad had to translate the text of the Polish document for the German border officials and they accepted it after a Soviet guard confirmed the accuracy of his translation. At 4 o'clock in the afternoon we finally received the necessary papers that permitted us to continue our travel to Bad Kissingen in Bavaria.

On the next day, March 22, we were able to catch a train that took us from Eisenach to the zonal border at Bebra, where we again transferred to another train which was operating only in the American occupation zone. Before boarding that train we had to undergo delousing, a fairly simple procedure of having insecticide powder blown into our clothes. After traveling much of the night and changing trains one more time, we arrived in Bad Kissingen in the morning of March 23. Today, after the reunification of Germany, it would take about six to seven hours to travel from Berlin to Bad Kissingen by train and less time by car. It took us four days in 1946.

Our relatives in Bad Kissingen consisted of one of my dad's cousins and his family. They had escaped from Lithuania in the summer of 1944 and, after a temporary stay in West Prussia and Saxony, had settled in Bavaria. Our arrival was not a big surprise to them for they were getting used to unannounced visits from relatives who were passing through. They were gracious to take us in for almost a week, while my parents hunted for a permanent place to settle. It was impossible to get a room let alone an apartment in the city. We were fortunate that Uncle Karl and his family and Aunt Alma had found refuge in Wollbach, a village over eight miles from Bad Kissingen. Here Aunt Alma had a small two-room apartment separate from Uncle Karl's family. One room of her small apartment happened to be vacant. Uncle Karl's daughter Alida had been staying there until she recently moved when her husband, a Lutheran pastor, was assigned a church in southern Bavaria after being discharged from an American prisoner of war camp. Aunt Ottilie joined Alida who was expecting her first child. During this time, Aunt Alma was taking care of her brother's household, and she came to her room only for the night so that we had more freedom in her apartment during the day. In short, all kinds of developments came together at a fortuitous time and afforded us accommodations that took us off the flight and travel route after many weeks.

As recent expellees from the eastern German territories we were among the very lucky ones. Our flight from Pomerania in early 1946 saved us from the massive German expulsion that followed later in the year and continued until 1947. Between 1945 and 1947 about twelve million Germans were forced out of the formerly German lands east of the Oder-Neisse line together with German minorities from Eastern Europe, Poland, Czechoslovakia, and Yugoslavia. They were pushed into a truncated Germany which had been reduced by one fourth of its pre-war territory. Their expulsion came under conditions often much worse than what we experienced. Early estimates indicated that over one and a half million German refugees and expellees died during this massive transfer of population, one of the several ethnic cleansings that occurred in Europe during the twentieth century. With the loss of the German territories east of the Oder-Neisse line Germany forfeited lands that had been German for seven hundred years. Its borders were pushed back to German-dominated regions in the Middle Ages. Such was the human and territorial price that was exacted from Germany because of Hitler's megalomania.

References

Blum, Arkadius, ed. *Unsere Familiengeschichte eingebettet in die Geschichte unseres Volkes und der Weltpolitik von 1731-1981.* Augsburg: J. Walch, 1983.

Benz, Wolfgang, ed. *Die Vertreibung der Deutschen aus dem Osten: Ursachen, Ereignisse, Folgen.* Frankfurt am Main: Fischer Taschenbuch Verlag, 1985.

Normann, Käthe von. *Tagebuch aus Pommern 1945-1946.* München: Deutscher Taschenbuch Verlag, 1962.

Zayas, Maurice de. *A Terrible Revenge: The Ethnic Cleansing of the East European Germans, 1944-1950.* New York: St. Martin's Press, 1994.

SEVEN

Gradual Return to Normalcy

Wollbach and Bad Kissingen

Once we landed in the American occupation zone of Germany, we immediately felt a greater sense of security, just as in West Berlin we had felt much less vulnerable than in the Soviet sector and the Soviet-occupied eastern Germany. We no longer had to fear being arrested, suddenly commandeered for some work detail, or worse, being deported. At that time, American soldiers did not take personal possessions from civilians at will or invade dwellings as they had in the first few days of occupation. Crimes perpetrated by occupation troops were isolated incidents. We saw American military personnel only in the city of Bad Kissingen, where there was an American army post. They came through the village of Wollbach very rarely on an excursion drive. In cities military police controlled road traffic and issued speeding tickets. People living in cities complained about having their houses confiscated by military personnel and not being able to get them released for years. In Bad Kissingen Americans also confiscated most of the hotels for their use which were normally available for resort guests when the city was operating as a health resort. It was a city that had been left unscathed during the Allied bombing attacks and thus offered desirable facilities and quarters for the American occupiers.

Our relatives helped us, having been settled for some months after escaping from eastern Germany. It took a little while for us to obtain ration cards and meet all the requirements to establish residence. Acquiring living accommodations and even some basic household necessities was daunting unless one knew someone willing to share a few things. Uncle Karl and Aunt Alma, my dad's siblings, were among the first to help. Aunt Alma who originally shared her two-room village apartment with Alida, her niece, gave us one room. I also remember how Aunt Olga Reinert, dad's sister, came several months later for a visit to Wollbach from the British occupation zone, where she and her relatives had landed after trekking many hundreds of miles. When she heard that we had lost all of our bedding, she brought some along for our use.

Native Bavarians often looked upon us as outsiders if not unwelcome intruders. They were not likely to share anything with refugee strangers. It usually took a while before they would warm up to more friendly relations. In villages they spoke their Bavarian dialect, which was difficult for us to understand. There was also a denominational divide as most newcomers were Protestant, while the natives in most regions of Bavaria were thoroughly Catholic. In predominantly Protestant areas of West Germany, the divide was the other way but there was probably more acceptance of Catholics by Protestants than of Protestants by Catholics in conservative Bavaria.

Our new one-room home had a wood stove but no indoor plumbing except a faucet with running water in the hallway. The lavatory was an outhouse at some distance in the backyard. The house sat on an open unfinished basement which had often more than just a puddle of water. My mother dubbed our dwelling "the villa on a frog pond." The narrow village street next to the house became a running brook during winter and spring floods when a small nearby stream overflowed. When we moved in, there was enough wood left to burn so that we could do all the cooking for meals and heat our dwelling satisfactorily. Once the summer came, my dad, Uncle Karl, and I joined other villagers in lugging logs for firewood from a forest at some distance from Wollbach to a nearby road from where a tractor-drawn wagon transported them to our yard. After that the logs had to be sawed into shorter pieces and split for ordinary firewood. Since all this had to be done by hand we all got plenty of exercise preparing for the following cold season. It was essential to have a good supply of firewood during the winter of 1946-47, for it set historic records of cold temperatures. That harsh winter was followed by an unusually hot and often humid summer.

As we settled in, one of the continuing challenges was to obtain enough food. All ordinary food items were rationed due to limited supply. In the American zone the average ration per person was officially 1200 calories a day, but in practice often less. In the British occupation zone the daily caloric intake was even lower during 1946-1947, sinking to 1000 calories, as reported in the news. With the influx of not just thousands but millions of German refugees from the former eastern Germany, Poland, Hungary, Czechoslovakia, and Yugoslavia, the number of consumers escalated in the western occupation zones of Germany and exacerbated the food shortages. To prevent starvation in West Germany, eventually food had to be imported from the United States and from Britain (where bread rationing was instituted for several years after the war). However despite these augmented food supplies large numbers of people suffered malnutrition. Though we were living in a rural area and had perhaps a better chance to obtain some additional food stuffs through barter with farmers, this was not really true of Wollbach, located in the Rhön region and known as the sandbox of northern Bavaria. The low agricultural productivity of the region made it difficult for many farmers to make a living, and often at least one breadwinner in the family sought employment in the city.

Our ration cards entitled us to limited grams of bread, flour, a small amount of potatoes, vegetables, meat, and a few grams of butter and cheese per week, never enough for adequate meals. The backyard of the house we stayed in had a small plot, and we tried to create a garden to grow a few vegetables. Since these had to be raised from seeds, one of the annoying interferences was some neighborhood chickens that invaded the garden to scratch for seeds. There was no good way of erecting a secure fence and a scarecrow certainly would not have deterred the pesky intruders. One vegetable that grew well was spinach. After these hungry years my mother almost never touched spinach again. In Vilkaviškis, our last residence in Lithuania, I had raised rabbits as pets; in rural Wollbach I kept some to supplement our meager meat rations. But just finding enough grass, dandelions, or scarce clover to feed them became a challenge. I gathered whatever sparse grass I could find in ditches alongside village roads. The adjoining fields belonging to farmers had good grass and clover, but I was disinclined to steal. To fatten the few rabbits would have required some grain, which was also not available. Other agricultural products were similarly very difficult to get in Wollbach. On one or two occasions my dad tried to get some potatoes from several village farmers, but could collect at the most only two or three potatoes (not pounds!). Our ration cards entitled us to buy some cigarettes, so my parents bought them even though no one in the family smoked. We found a young man in the village who was eager to trade eggs for cigarettes, and that barter arrangement netted an egg or two from time to time.

Our food conditions would have been even more desperate, if it hadn't been for American food (and clothing) parcels that started arriving from time to time after the fall of 1946. In late 1945 or early 1946 several of our relatives had reestablished contact by letter with Aunt Emilie Fischer in Minneapolis and Aunt Anna Kasewurm in Westfield, Massachusetts, who had immigrated to the United States before World War I. Both of the American aunts were sisters of my dad and four other siblings - Uncle Karl Blum, Aunt Wanda Blum Aunt Alma Schulz, and Aunt Olga Reinert. Both American aunts had kept in fairly regular contact with their brothers and sisters in Lithuania and briefly in Germany until Pearl Harbor in December 1941 ended all correspondence.

It was especially Aunt Emilie, widowed in 1946 and without children of her own, who earned our lasting admiration and gratitude for providing most of the help with food and clothing parcels. She packed the gift parcels on her dining room table and then sent them off to the many relatives in Germany. Even though she collected some items from relatives on her late husband's side, she spent quite a bit of her own modest income to buy cans of food and occasionally even some new clothing. Some other relatives and their own grown children also helped from time to time by either sending their own parcels or paying money to CARE or other organizations that sent prepared food packages. Some of these early food parcels were actually food provisions originally prepared for American troops. These also contained some American cigarettes, which very quickly replaced the devalued German currency and were traded for food or consumer goods outside the rationed supply. However, this kind of barter stoked the black market in the American occupation zone, and soon American cigarettes and sometimes even coffee were barred from gift parcels coming from the States to Germany. Germans were also not allowed to have any dollars at that time and thus Americans could not help their relatives and friends with money. For us everything we received from America was welcome but it was especially lard, spam, and some other products that contained fat which were essential for our nutrition. Even so, my dad developed symptoms of malnutrition during these difficult two years. In the immediate years after the war, the American authorities censored the correspondence that we received from relatives and others in the States, and we found that entire lines had been cut from practically every letter. Since usually both sides of the letter paper had written text, we received often only fragmented messages.

With the overflow of refugees from the East, the depressed postwar economic conditions made it more and more difficult for newcomers to find any employment in many areas of western Germany unless they had special skills that were in demand. If there were job openings, the natives generally favored natives in the hiring, frequently discriminating against newcomers. In rural areas, the kind of employment that was most available was work on farms. My dad volunteered to help the local village clerk in her office without pay since he had bookkeeping skills.

Prospects of gainful employment opened up for my dad when he got in touch with one of his former seminary teachers; he recommended him to the Methodist district superintendent in charge of northern Bavaria and Württemberg. It turned out that a pastor was needed for the small Schweinfurt and Würzburg congregations to fill in for the regular minister who had become ill. So starting in the fall of 1946 and continuing through the summer of 1947, my father commuted to these cities on weekends and sometimes also during the week to conduct services, usually at the homes of some congregation members. Both of these cities had been heavily bombed during Anglo-American air raids and showed the scars of severe destruction for years to come. Generally, it was not difficult getting regular trains from Bad Kissingen to Schweinfurt and to Würzburg, but getting from Wollbach to Bad Kissingen and back was more complicated since bus service was limited. On several occasions my dad had to hitchhike or even walk eight or so miles. Fortunately, this assignment was short term. When the South German Methodist Conference, the regional representative body of the Methodist Church, held its annual meeting in the summer of 1947, he was appointed as regular pastor to a church in Cottenweiler, not far from Stuttgart in Württemberg.

At age fourteen I was too young to look for work, even though I had to register with the Bad Kissingen state employment office to remain eligible for a ration card. It did not appear practical for me to return to school during the few remaining months of the school year of 1945-46, and I waited until the late summer 1946 to resume school at the beginning of the new school term. Before school ended for me in December 1944 my weakest subject was English, since I had to make up a year of it at that time. So I simply studied on my own during the spring and summer of 1946, learning as much as I could from one or two beginner's books that my mother or I found in a bookstore. I was surprised to discover upon returning to the academic high school in Bad Kissingen that after missing almost two years of formal schooling I was able to keep up with my classmates in English. But I had a new challenge, a second foreign language, Latin was required. My classmates had already had almost a full year of it and so I had to make it up during the early months of the new school term. This time I did not have a tutor to help. The Latin teacher simply handed me the Latin textbook that he used in his class and said: "You start with the first lesson and work your way through the book as quickly as you can." After two or three months, he began to call on me in class and expected me to follow the lessons of my classmates. With occasional help from my cousin Erwin in Wollbach, who had had some Latin in high school many years before, I made fairly good progress and was pretty much in step with my classmates toward the end of spring 1947. In the other subjects I had no particular difficulties, except temporarily in algebra. But this also passed, when one of my second cousins in Bad Kissingen explained to me some of the basic rules of beginning algebra, which I had never been taught before.

School administrations in south Germany assumed that students would return with varying levels of preparation after the war, having often missed regular schooling for some length of time. In Bavaria this problem was dealt with in secondary schools by having every student repeat the grade that he or she had been enrolled in before schooling was interrupted. On the other hand, in the neighboring state of Württemberg to which I transferred in the late summer of 1947, the educational ministry simply added an additional school year to the academic secondary curriculum. I was enrolled in grade three of the then eight-year academic high school in Bad Kissingen. The high school in Zuckau, West Prussia, that I had attended previously was a middle school since it lacked the three upper grades of ordinary academic high schools. All the other secondary schools that I enrolled in were regular academic high schools and called Oberschule or Oberrealschule. When I returned to West Germany in 1963, eleven years after my emigration to the United States, I discovered that all of them had been renamed Gymnasium, a designation which had a historic ring and origin in German secondary education. At the end of eight years (in Bavaria) or nine years (in Württemberg), a graduate of these schools had to pass a rigorous examination to obtain his or her Abitur, the prerequisite for admission to a university.

The logistics of my getting to school from Wollbach to Bad Kissingen every weekday, including Saturday, was sometimes complicated. I was the only student from a group of villages who commuted to Bad Kissingen to attend the academic high school. An early morning bus transported workers to the city and returned them in the late afternoon but the owner/driver of the worker bus always insisted that he could only take additional passengers if there was room left after all the workers had boarded. Nonworkers always had to wait until the regular worker passengers had gotten on the bus. When finally full, the coach was crowded with passengers having to stand in the aisle and at the front of the cabin. To ensure that I would have a fair chance to catch a ride, my dad from time to time had to "encourage" the owner/driver to take me along by visiting him at his home and passing a cigar or some other item from American gift packages to him. I almost always got on the bus going to Bad Kissingen, but there were also some unusual days - worker holidays that were not school holidays, or when workers complained there were too many extra riders - when I had to walk back from Bad Kissingen or borrow my cousin Erwin's bike.

On Saturday mornings, because of later departure, I could not get into town on time for school by bus but I usually could get a ride back in the early afternoon. So on Friday evenings I would stay over at the home of my dad's cousin, Aunt Anna Freitag. Here I also frequently did my homework after school in the afternoon on other weekdays before I caught the bus to go home. I have some happy memories of those Friday stayovers because my two second cousins, Martha and Alfons Freitag, and I quite regularly went to a movie in the evening. It was difficult to get tickets right before the evening performance but by lining up in the afternoon I always came back with tickets in hand. Since both of my cousins worked during the day, they would have otherwise often missed the movies. Most of the films offered happy escapes from work, school, and life in those difficult postwar days. There were Viennese stories of known musicians, some American and British films of that time, and, for us, a first exposure to several Charlie Chaplin classics. My mother always sent an army mess dish along with some soup, quite often some fruit soup, which I could warm up on the stove for my supper. This was enough to keep body and soul together, though I could have eaten more. The company of my second cousins and the entertainment we enjoyed and remembered for years made up for whatever cares we had at the time.

I remember the summer of 1947 as unusually hot with temperatures around 100 degrees Fahrenheit with high humidity on some days. Since German schools continued into July, affording us only a six-week summer vacation, I took to the city swimming pool on several afternoons after school. Here I also often met some of my classmates. This was a chance for some socializing until I had to catch my bus going home. While in Wollbach, I did not make any friends. I had little in common with the local farm boys, and since they spoke a dialect I could not even understand too well, I was marked as an outsider. Usually on my own, I attended some village soccer games of the young adults and also took in a few of the local amateur plays, some with strangely religious content, which were performed in a village hall or in larger homes. It was different in school, where there was a mixture of natives and refugees and we all communicated in High German. Whatever other socializing I did was mostly with my much older cousin Erwin and occasionally visiting second cousins, all of whom were also older than I. When the time came, leaving Wollbach was not difficult since I had not established any roots there. After the summer vacation of 1947, I reported to the Bad Kissingen school only on the first day to indicate that I was transferring to the Backnang Oberschule. The principal's office provided a transfer form and a transcript with my grades for the preceding year, and I was on my way to my next postwar school adventure.

Cottenweiler and Schwäbisch Hall

The move to Cottenweiler, a larger village several miles from the even larger town Backnang and known as the "south German tanner town," changed our lives mostly for the better. Backnang was conveniently located on a railroad line on which one could reach Stuttgart, the well known German city, in about forty minutes. When we stayed overnight at the home of a congregation member in Schweinfurt while transferring to a train toward Backnang, our host predicted that our living standard in Württemberg, especially in nutrition, would improve markedly. He was right. We left the sandbox of the Rhön for a richer farm country with no regrets.

Living in the more prosperous farming region of Württemberg gave us access to enough bread, potatoes, vegetables, and fruit so that we could have good substantive meals that satisfied the appetite. One of the congregation members gave us her bread ration cards, saying that she did not need them. In early October, it was customary for the farmer members of the congregation to bring samples of their produce to the annual Sunday harvest thanksgiving service, which was traditionally observed in Germany. At the end, the minister was allowed to keep these contributions. There was also a garden that belonged to the parsonage where we could raise some produce of our own. In June 1948, the currency reform in West Germany ended the rationing system and now it was simply one's income which determined the individual's or family's standard of living. In contrast to respectable salaries paid to German Lutheran pastors, classified as civil servants and supported by a mandatory church tax, Free Church Methodist ministerial salaries were sustained only by free will contributions of parishioners and were therefore meager. However it helped that we had free housing in the parsonage. For the first two years in Cottenweiler we had only two rooms, since the regular minister's apartment on the second floor of the parsonage continued to be occupied by the former pastor's widow and her two children. Her husband had not returned from the war and it took the district superintendent several years to find alternate accommodations for this hardship situation. The rooms that we occupied were normally for church functions, but they could not be used for this purpose until our third year in Cottenweiler when we moved into the vacated upstairs parsonage.

All the Cottenweiler church services and Sunday school were held in the church hall that was attached to the parsonage. There were also three or four congregation branches several miles away in neighboring villages where my dad conducted Sunday evening and often midweek prayer services in members' homes. To get to these places, my dad had to walk since public transportation to them did not exist or was not convenient for the times needed. The church owned a bicycle used by the previous minister, but my dad never mastered the skill of riding a bike and so he remained dependent on his shoe soles. However, the bicycle did not stand idle. I loved to explore the nearby regions on long bike rides the first few months on Sunday afternoons, and I also used it for church youth excursions and on rare occasions to get to school or some school related events. Before the currency reform of 1948 new bicycles were not available and afterward they were very expensive. Even used bikes commanded highly inflated prices.

After arriving in Cottenweiler, I was ready to resume school and quickly enrolled at the Oberschule of Backnang, about eight miles from Cottenweiler. To get there I had to walk about a mile to the next small township to catch a bus to the city. In contrast to Wollbach, there was a sizable group of students from the various villages that attended a vocationally oriented middle school and a smaller number that was enrolled at the academic high school in Backnang. Upon enrollment in its fourth grade, I had another surprise. Latin was not offered as the second foreign language in this academic secondary school, but this time instead French was required. I needed to make up almost two years of it! By now I was quite experienced in doing remedial foreign language work in order to catch up with my classmates. Fortunately, I was not the only student who lacked French; there were three or four of us. With the help of the kindly elderly French teacher who tutored us for several months for free, I managed to catch up in about three or four months with my classmates. Granted the progress of the entire class was not overly rapid, since we had French class periods only twice a week. The proficiency in English was more demanding and we had more frequent lessons during the week. In other subjects, German, mathematics, history, religion, biology, I was pretty well in step.

In grades five and six instruction in physics and chemistry were added to our curriculum. Even though the expectations were high, it was not overly difficult to maintain a B or B- overall average. Straight A students in the German academic high schools that I attended after the war were a rarity and none existed in my classes. My interest lay definitely in the humanities, especially foreign languages, literature, and history, even though in the early years of mathematics and sciences I enjoyed most of these subjects too and got quite good grades. Chemistry interested me the least.

Every year our class lost a few students who dropped out because of low grades or to start working; many entered an apprenticeship. They usually had reached the age at which full time school attendance was no longer required. I considered doing the same to start a business apprenticeship for which I had been accepted in Waiblingen, a town about fifteen miles from Backnang. When I had asked for a recommendation from one of my teachers, he had discouraged me from pursuing the apprenticeship, saying that I should stay in school and consider eventual university studies, but I told him my parents did not have the means to help me with education beyond high school. Working one's way through a university was not as common then and realistic in Germany as it became later on. When my dad tried to arrange for my living accommodations in Waiblingen through a ministerial colleague, there was a delay; whereupon the prospective employer filled the position with someone else. At first, I was disappointed but in the end it was the best thing that could have happened, for it would have changed the professional course of my life.

In secondary school, a major weeding point came for all of us at the end of the sixth year when we had to take comprehensive written examinations in German, mathematics, English and French, and pass an oral examination in biology. I prepared for several months for these tests. I passed almost all of the examinations with a B and received a commendation. About half of the class of 34 students elected to drop out at the end of the school year without taking the comprehensives, including all but one of the girls. Of those of us who took the comprehensive exams, I think, only one actually failed.

There were no organized extracurricular activities after school except for an end-of-school party which we six-year students arranged. Several of our teachers came to this party and found themselves roasted by clever poems and recitations composed by several of my classmates. The little socializing I did with school friends during the year was in Backnang after school in town or occasionally at someone's parents' home. Of that time Günther Seitter and I have remained good friends and in contact until the present. I often stopped at the American library across from our school to look at German and American magazines and, occasionally, to borrow American books. Such libraries were established by the American occupation authorities in major towns to expose interested Germans to American publications and American life. Among my classmates, none had a steady part time job. Such jobs were difficult to get and it was not really customary for students of our age to work except perhaps to help out in a family business. I remember only one fellow student who earned some money working part time during one vacation to finance a hobby. Since homework was always demanding in the higher grades, we did not have much free time to begin with.

Most of my extracurricular pursuits centered on church related activities. There was no organized church youth group but a number of us teens and young adults occasionally visited events at nearby Methodist churches or took bike rides to woods and lakes for picnics. Also on certain Sunday afternoons during the summer, my father conducted outdoor services at one or the other of the church branches in nearby villages to which the entire congregation was always invited. I sang in the small church choir, as did my mother, learned to play the euphonium (tenor horn) for the church brass choir, and taught myself to play the harmonium, the main instrument accompanying the congregation during services. I never reached enough proficiency to master advanced music but could play church hymns, folk songs, and other simple pieces. One book that I used for my harmonium practice and especially enjoyed contained arias and short interludes from operatic literature. I also liked chorales Johann Sebastian Bach had harmonized, for they were part of Germany's outstanding church music heritage. And best of all, they were usually not too complicated and I could play most of them tolerably well after some practice.

There were few concerts presented in Backnang, but through school I was exposed to opera. From time to time the school received several student tickets to attend the Stuttgart Opera. I was usually lucky enough to get one. In school every week we had music instruction and the teacher always spent considerable time introducing those of us who had tickets to the music and story of the featured opera. These were top-notch productions in which several of Germany's opera stars of that time like Wolfgang Windgassen, his father Fritz, and Dietrich Fischer-Dieskau performed. The first opera that I remember attending in Stuttgart was Carl Maria von Weber's *Freischütz*. It left a lasting impression on me. Others that followed included Mozart's *Abduction from the Seraglio, Magic Flute*, Wagner's *Flying Dutchman,* and Verdi's *Aida*. These experiences sparked my lifelong enjoyment of opera.

The Methodist church had the custom of moving its ministers every few years. These decisions were usually made by the bishop's cabinet at the annual summer meeting of the regional church conference. This became a stressful time for ministers' families, since they often did not know how long they might continue where they were situated. My father's turn came at the end of his third year in Cottenweiler. At first he was to be transferred to another rural church in Württemberg remote from a city, which would have made it very difficult for me to continue my high school education. The pastor of the Backnang Methodist church with whom my father had regularly exchanged pulpits intervened on my behalf so the bishop's cabinet relented and arranged for a direct exchange of the ministers of Schwäbisch Hall and Cottenweiler. In the fall 1950, I transferred to the Oberrealschule in Schwäbisch Hall when my father was moved from the Cottenweiler church to the Methodist church in that city.

The church parsonage in Schwäbisch Hall was located on the second floor of a three story building that had two other apartments. The minister's apartment had ample rooms so that I had a room of my own for the first time in my life. A hall on the first floor served as the assembly hall for the church. Though Schwäbisch Hall had suffered only minor war damage, the building across from the Methodist building had been hit by a bomb and demolished. Five years after the end of the war, the outer façade of the Methodist church building still showed the unrepaired bomb damage.

The Methodist congregation in Schwäbisch Hall was fairly small. My father was glad to have some contact with another Free Church pastor at the Evangelical United Brethren Church and one of the pastors of the main Lutheran church in the city. There were three or four Lutheran congregations in Schwäbisch Hall because the region became thoroughly Protestant during the Reformation of the 16th century. I found living in this medieval city, rich in history and culture, exhilarating. Its size at that time was over 20,000, similar to that of Backnang, but the atmosphere and cultural opportunities were more cosmopolitan than what I had experienced before.

As a member of the minister's family I was expected to be involved in my father's congregation, and I tried to make things easier for my dad. No one in the congregation played the harmonium to accompany the singing of hymns in the services, and so, on short notice, I became the regular accompanist. My mother might have done some of that, but she was more out of practice than I. I also took on the task of conducting the small church choir. My natural talent in music is definitely limited and I did not feel comfortable in that role, but I tried to further my command of basic music through self-study and practice. Two young adult church members played the violin so we played together just for our own enjoyment and for occasional presentations in church. My two favorite extracurricular activities were reading classical pieces of German literature and attending as many musical concerts as I could as long as they were free. Schwäbisch Hall offered many small ensemble concerts and also vocal artist recitals. Through them I was exposed to music by Béla Bartók, Paul Hindemith, and other contemporaries for the first time. 1950, the bicentennial year of Johann Sebastian Bach's death, was observed by a great many concerts. They were presented at the local St. Michael's Church, the architectural hallmark of Schwäbisch Hall, including a Sunday evening organ recital series of the master's entire organ works. I managed to attend all of them, and I also remember a fine performance of Bach's Christmas Oratorio that my mother and I attended.

School became again my main activity. The transition in school was fairly smooth. My new classmates were quite congenial, but I did not stay at the school long enough to establish close lasting friendships. Since I came with only two foreign languages, English and French, I was automatically put in the math-science track, which had a heavy emphasis on physics, chemistry, even some basics of meteorology, and higher mathematics, including analytical geometry and early calculus. Even though I managed to keep in step more or less, the emphasis on mathematics and sciences with attendant demanding homework began to wear, since I really liked to spend more time with German literature and the English and French languages. So at the end of the seventh grade I made the decision to transfer into the humanities track of the school, which required Latin as a third foreign language. In that curriculum, I continued in advanced mathematics and in the sciences, but with less time devoted to these subjects. Well, I had had some Latin but not nearly enough, since at this school humanities students had had at least five years of it. I tried very hard to catch up during the six-week summer vacation in 1951, but had a rather dreadful time in the fall finding my way into Cicero, Virgil, and other Latin classics.

I was spared continuing Latin nightmares when in December

1951 my parents and I received immigration visas for the United States, and I was able to drop out of high school altogether. Another subject during the fall term that had baffled some of my classmates and me was a course in philosophy. Unfortunately, we did not have a textbook and the presentations of the teacher were at times too rambling to make much sense of this new subject. I left before having to take a test in that course, which I certainly did not miss. However I learned to appreciate and understand philosophy in my first and second year in college.

It was during my time in Schwäbisch Hall that I developed a better understanding of the merits of democracy and its uses in government and society. I had an interesting teacher in German and English, a retired old major who had also worked with a Nazi organization for Germans abroad during the Third Reich. He shared some of his political views in class. His full title was Professor Dr. Krehl. The designation "professor" had been acquired by some of the older Gymnasium teachers but was only used primarily in Württemberg, as far as I know. Otherwise the title was reserved for university level teachers. As several of my classmates told me, Professor Krehl and one other teacher of mine had only recently been amnestied, and allowed to return to their profession. When the Americans after the war tried to arrest the ex-major, he had managed to escape and hide out for three years somewhere in northwestern Germany. He was a German conservative and patriot who had not fully come to terms with democracy as a desirable system of government but appreciated certain aspects of it. He thought the Americans and British had made a major mistake at the end of the war in 1945 by not allying with the Germans against the Russians to push them out of Europe. Obviously he had little grasp of the fact that American public opinion would have never supported such a turnabout against an ally in the war after Hitler's defeat.

Starting in the late fall 1950, the local American authorities in

Schwäbisch Hall made efforts to reach out to interested local German civilians by establishing a weekly forum for conversation. It was all in American English and a grand opportunity for those of us who attended these forums to improve our English conversational skills as well as to learn more about America. This group attracted primarily upper high school age youths who already had a good command of English literature and vocabulary from school. For several months American civilian and military personnel participated in these meetings and offered presentations on aspects of American life and, in the case of the military, on what was happening in the Korean War. Later the local American Resident Officer, a civilian, replaced the formal U.S. military occupation authority (though the American troops remained) and carried on these weekly conversation meetings throughout much of 1951, quite often at his home. Seven or eight of us high school students were regular attendees and we not only became fluent in conversational English but also learned quite a bit about recent American history, attitudes, cultural affairs, democratic institutions, and practices. In exchange our American host heard quite a bit from us what Germans were thinking. I always look back with happy memories upon these get-togethers, which prepared me well for my immigration to the States.

EIGHT

Leaving Germany

Emigration

Since my dad's two sisters, Aunts Anna Kasewurm and Emilie Fischer, had immigrated to the States several years before World War I and had found a settled existence in the New World away from wars and revolution in Europe, my father had for years been thinking of also leaving the homeland if the opportunity ever presented itself. As far as I know, he did not actively explore the possibility before the outbreak of World War II. The Great Depression that affected both the States and Europe during the 1930s did not bode well for an easier existence in the United States or Canada. Once the war broke out the struggle for survival on the Old Continent shelved any plans for a new life outside Europe.

After the war and our flight from Soviet-occupied eastern Germany in 1945, we were fortunate to enjoy relative normalcy because my father was able to return to the Methodist ministry. Still, conditions in West Germany during the late forties and early fifties were difficult, especially with the postwar influx of millions of expellees from former German lands and German refugees from Eastern Europe into what was left of Germany. Most of them ended up in the already densely populated West German areas, enormously exacerbating the housing shortage and unemployment. Many millions of newcomers in West Germany faced an uncertain future. In 1951 the unemployment rate was 8 to 9 per cent and at least one third of the two million West German unemployed were expellees and refugees. By 1958 West Germany had to absorb over nine million displaced Germans from the former eastern Germany and Eastern Europe and more than three million others from Germany's Soviet-occupied zone. While my father was in the ministry he received several letters from German refugees from Lithuania, begging him to help them relocate to south Germany, since they were living in areas of northern Germany like Schleswig Holstein where economic opportunities were practically nonexistent.

Eventually the recovery and expansion of the West German economy started with the assistance of Marshall Plan aid in the late forties. Full implementation of the social market economy in the fifties very markedly improved living and working conditions for most West Germans, old and new. The expellees and refugees played a significant role in the West German economic resurgence of the fifties by providing an essential pool of skilled and unskilled labor for the economic expansion. History books now call this the Economic Miracle of Germany. The Equalization of the Burden Act of 1952 helped many refugees and expellees recover some of their material losses. It provided limited compensation for lost property, homes, businesses, and assets. This fund which compensated the displaced Germans was raised from a special tax on West German assets and from supplements to the federal budget. The special tax was stretched over thirty years so that it would not become too onerous a burden for those who had to pay it. All this happened after our emigration so that we did not benefit from the West German sharing of the postwar burden.

My parents' economic recovery was slow and difficult, since they had lost all their personal possessions at the end of the war and during our flight. Their financial future looked bleak because my father would have had to retire less than ten years after he resumed the full time ministry in 1947. Since he had spent most of his years in the ministry in a non-German Methodist conference and no funds survived the war to support retired pastors, he would not have had enough years of service credit in the German Methodist church to provide an adequate pension. Pastors in German Free churches, in contrast to the state-supported Lutheran Church, were paid low salaries during their active years of service though also provided with free housing. However, once such servants of the church retired their pensions were very low, and there was not much subsidized church housing available. My parents would not have been able to live on what my father was projected to receive after age 65, the mandatory retirement age. The concern for the future was very much on my parents' minds. Though immigration to the United States meant starting a new life in a foreign country, it seemed the only opportunity to escape the painful recovery and reconstruction in Germany. My parents also thought that opportunities for continuing my education beyond secondary school and finding a suitable profession in the United States were more promising than in Germany.

Yet, wanting to leave Germany was one thing and being able to immigrate to the United States was quite a different matter. It took us several years. In the postwar years, immigration to the States was generally possible under an immigration law of 1924, but there were yearly quotas based on national origin from Britain, Germany, Italy, and other European countries. The 1890 census had been used to determine the nationality distribution in the States and so quotas favored Western Europeans and discriminated against eastern and southeastern Europeans. Even though the German quota was probably the second largest (after Britain's), it was quickly filled by the backlog of persons from the war and its aftermath. When my parents inquired about the prospects of immigrating to the U.S. in 1948, they were told that the German quota was presumed to be full for many years ahead and therefore their chances were very poor. Many next of kin and other hardship family situations were given priority.

In the fall 1948 my father and I had opportunity to meet with Bishop Raymond Wade, the prewar bishop of the Baltic and central European Methodist churches, and a representative of the American Methodist Board of Missions, when they were visiting West Germany to learn firsthand about the state of the Methodist churches. With my limited school English I tried to translate for my dad. These men at that time could also offer no encouragement regarding immigration. Bishop Wade had been reassigned to the Indiana area after leaving Europe in 1939 and was trying to find pastorates for some of the displaced non-German ministers from the Baltic States in different areas of the U.S. A prerequisite was naturally a reasonable command of English, which my father did not have at that time. Many other barriers also stood in the way. It was several years before more Germans were admitted to the U.S. beyond the annual German immigration quota.

At the end of World War II, Germany was inundated with over seven million foreigners from other parts of Europe who were stranded there, nearly all of them in the three West German occupation zones. Most of them had been brought to central Europe as forced workers by the Nazi regime for the German war machine. In the immediate years after the hostilities ended, most of these Displaced Persons (DPs) were repatriated to their homelands but a fairly large number refused to return to their communist eastern European countries. Many were Jews who had survived the Holocaust, including Jews who fled from postwar Poland where they faced renewed persecution under the communist regime. By mid-1947 well over six hundred thousand Displaced Persons were still in the western zones of Germany and Austria, usually housed in temporary camps. Over half of them were in the American zone.

At that same time western Germany also had to cope with the influx of millions of German expellees and refugees. At the Potsdam Conference in 1945, the United States and Britain had accepted a Soviet proposal to expel all remaining Germans from the German territories (to be annexed by Poland and the Soviet Union) east of the Oder-Neisse line. Also, ethnic Germans from Poland, Czechoslovakia, Hungary, and Yugoslavia either fled or were forced to leave their homelands. As a result, over twelve million people fled from these areas or moved to the geographically shrunk postwar Germany. A majority of them ended up in the American, British, and, to a lesser extent, French occupation zones.

While the gigantic transfer of people was underway, the Western Allies and other free European nations paid little or no attention to the problems of German expellees and refugees. But by 1947 these powers concluded that the best solution for a permanent accommodation of non-German DPs who could not or did not want to be repatriated was to resettle them outside Germany. For this purpose, the United Nations, with the support of the United States, Canada, Australia, and several western European countries, established the International Refugee Organization (IRO) after the United Nations Relief and Rehabilitation Administration (UNRRA) had been dissolved in June 1947. Such a program could only succeed, if the major member nations agreed to accept substantial numbers of the Displaced Persons for permanent residence. To this end, Displaced Persons measures were enacted by Canada, Australia, and the United States, and between 1948 and 1952 over 700,000 DPs found new permanent homes away from the troubled European continent.

President Truman tried to initiate a United States policy regarding Displaced Persons in 1945, but it required several years before the Displaced Persons Act was passed in June 1948 due to heavy resistance in Congress. Many congressional members took a restrictionist stance in the admission of large numbers of immigrants to the United States. The President signed the DP Act reluctantly. The final version authorized the admission of 200,000 DPs during the following two years, which he supported, but the act favored Balts, who constituted a small portion of the total DP population, and agricultural workers, while discriminating against Jews and others from Eastern Europe of largely urban backgrounds. Another restrictive feature that affected Jews, many Poles, and Yugoslavs most was the requirement that DPs had to have entered one of the western zones on or before December 22, 1945.

Over 27,000 ethnic Germans who had been born in Poland, Czechoslovakia, Hungary, Rumania, or Yugoslavia were also authorized to enter the United States under this act. Their numbers were however limited to 50 per cent of the existing German and Austrian immigration quotas.

Pressures in America soon mounted to liberalize the restrictive features of the Displaced Persons Act of 1948, especially its bias against Jewish and Catholic Displaced Persons. In June 1950, President Truman signed the second Displaced Persons Act into law, as resistance in Congress had weakened under public pressure. The American public showed more sympathy for refugees from Eastern Europe as the Cold War and persecution behind the Iron Curtain intensified. Under the amended Displaced Persons Act the total number of DPs to be admitted to the States was doubled to over 400,000, and included 18,000 Polish army veterans, 10,000 Greek refugees, 4000 European refugees from China, several other groups of Displaced Persons, and - most important to us - close to 55,000 ethnic Germans transferred from areas outside the reduced Germany. The cut-off date for Displaced Persons having entered the western zones was changed from 1945 to January 1, 1949, and the final deadline for issuing visas under the act was extended to December 31, 1951 (Loescher and Scanlan 19-22; Divine 130-142).

Thus a window of opportunity opened for my family to enter the United States when the amended Displaced Persons Act of 1950's definition of ethnic Germans was broadened to allow Germans from any area east of the Oder-Neisse line to immigrate to the States. I do not remember when my parents formally applied for immigration but for some time we had the important personal documents like birth and baptismal certificates, and the marriage certificate of my parents ready in the original and in English translation. In late

October 1951 my parents were notified to report for immigration processing in Hanau, a city near Frankfurt, in early November. At the time I was visiting my cousin Emil and his family in Munich and learned of the summons only on my return home. My father, on short notice, had to make arrangements to have at least two Sunday services covered during his absence and I had to miss school for the processing that lasted almost two weeks.

The immigration processing was arduous, lengthy, and frustrating, filled with rising hope but also the possibility of rejection. It entailed extensive background checks, including life and employment history, skills inventory, a comprehensive medical check to rule out infectious diseases, and an assessment of work fitness. We had to present proof from police authorities of having no criminal record and had to pass the records check of the Berlin Document Center to rule out membership in major Nazi organizations. I remember also answering a questionnaire that asked whether I had ever belonged to any of a huge list of organizations. At the time, I did not recognize any of their names, given in English and then not always well translated into German. Later I learned that these were mostly communist or radical leftist organizations. In September 1950 the Internal Security Act had been enacted over President Truman's veto, which gave the federal government extensive authority to screen aliens and exclude all subversives, including present and former members of the communist party.

During an interview with a CIC (Counter Intelligence Corps) officer, I was not asked any questions about my association with communist organizations. But as a nineteen-year-old German, I was suspected of having had some association with the Hitler Youth. Since at that time American immigration authorities were intent on excluding persons from entry into the States who had been significantly involved in Nazi organizations, had been Nazi collaborators, or had held positions that led them to commit criminal acts, there was also extensive probing of such associations of DP immigration applicants. I freely admitted my mandatory membership in the ten-to-fourteen-year-old Jungvolk formation of the Hitler Youth and told the interrogator about the kinds of activities I was involved in. My mother later mentioned that she was also asked about my participation in the Hitler Youth, presumably to corroborate the truthfulness of my statements. I don't know if there was much said during the CIC interview of my father's membership in the German Labor Front. By that time, I am sure, American interrogators knew that every employed German during the Nazi years generally had to pay dues to the German Labor Front. All these checks were very important and failure to measure up to the criteria of the Immigration Authority prevented entry into the States. I remember one young Russian that went through the processing with us who was rejected because he had served in the Soviet Army during the war.

An absolutely crucial requirement of the American DP immigration program was the so-called "assurance" or affidavit, a promise of an American sponsor to provide employment for a DP immigrant and housing for his or her family. Immigrants had to swear a 'Good Faith Oath' which obliged them to fulfill the terms of employment and housing provided by the private American sponsor. In practice this meant that the DPs were to spend a length of time working under the provisions of the specific sponsorship. This arrangement was basically a moral obligation rather than a legal one. In contrast, DP immigrants to Australia and Canada entered into a contractual agreement with the government or a governmental agency. In Australia this entailed a two-year obligation for the DPs and in Canada one year. Anyone violating these agreements was to be subject to deportation. For our immigration to the States, my Aunt Emilie Fischer in Minneapolis served as our sponsor. She had been widowed in 1946 but as the owner of a fourplex she could make a convincing case that she needed someone to help her care for her property. This was to be the "employment" for my dad, and she also provided a home for us to stay in. In fact, she very generously took us into her own home during the first two years. She had to cover the cost of our travel and transport of baggage that we were permitted to bring to the States from New York, the port of our entry, to Minneapolis. The expense of the boat fare from Germany to New York was assumed by the International Refugee Organization.

While we were waiting in a state of uncertainty for the immigration processing in Hanau to end, we had occasion to make a visit to nearby Frankfurt over one weekend. This was the first time for me and my mother to see the city where my father had spent three years at the Methodist Theological Seminary in the early twenties. There were still reminders of the destruction of the city from Allied bombing raids but much had also been reconstructed. We visited the Seminary and even had a chance to talk to the director, Dr. Friedrich Wunderlich, who soon thereafter became the bishop of the German Methodist Church after the death of Bishop Ernst Sommer. Aside from seeing the facilities of the Seminary, my more vivid memory of this visit was Director Wunderlich's effort to encourage me to enter the Methodist ministry. I did not say no outright but was politely noncommittal, because I had long since decided I would never follow my father into the ministry. As the prospect of emigration became a reality, I began to regret that I would leave the German Oberrealschule without obtaining my Abitur, the German high school diploma. On the other hand, I was able to enter the States under my father's sponsorship, since I was under 21. If I had been of age I would have needed a separate sponsor for my immigration. After finishing the processing in Hanau, we were informed that our application for immigration to the States had been approved. I remember a fair number of families who were denied immigration even though they seemed to be quite eligible on first sight. After prolonged waiting, it was a great relief to have certainty in our future though mingled with apprehension about yet another leap into the unknown. The next step for us who were now approved immigrants was to receive our American immigration visas, which were promised in three to four weeks. Following that, we were told, there would be a further delay before we could embark for the Atlantic crossing in Bremerhaven, an American enclave in the former British occupation zone.

We returned to Schwäbisch Hall from the immigration processing and began planning for our departure without knowing when that might be. As promised, our immigration visas arrived on time and we could now make concrete plans. Christmas vacation was just around the corner and I considered that a good time to drop out of school. My father's district superintendent had to make plans to cover his church once my dad left his pulpit. Only a limited amount of baggage was allowed; some of it was to be shipped and hand luggage was to be carried with us. Since we had lost everything in worldly goods except what we were able to carry during our flight from eastern Germany and had not acquired many new possessions, we did not have to bother with disposing mountains of belongings.

In late January we were notified to report for embarkation in Bremerhaven. It was set for the "early weeks of February," but no specific date was given. Unofficially we learned that the U.S. government used troop ships that brought GIs to Europe to take immigrants back to the States. The date of sailing was probably determined by the number of immigrants available to fill a ship's capacity. The entire cost of the transport was covered by the International Refugee Organization of the United Nations. Generally, there was a delay of one to two weeks after their report date before immigrants boarded a ship. A few days before we left Schwäbisch Hall, Aunt Olga Reinert and my cousins Emil and Albin came for a short farewell visit, literally between trains. This was the last time that my parents saw them, since they never had occasion to return to Germany for a visit.

We arrived in Bremerhaven more than a week before our actual embarkation date. Beyond some formalities we also had some free time to visit Bremen. Aunt Wanda Blum came from a town not too far away in northwestern Germany to say goodbye and wish us well in our immigration adventure. Younger male adults were required to sign up for some kind of work on board ship and to indicate what skills they possessed. The unofficial explanation for using passengers as workers on board ship was that the crew had been reduced to a skeleton. My father was exempt from this service. I indicated that I had typing skills and could work in an office.

On February 21, a Thursday, we were bussed to the harbor for our embarkation. Together with about 1200 other passengers we boarded the S.S. General Taylor in the afternoon and set out to sea in the evening. This was my first time on a large ship, and I wondered what lay ahead, having heard many stories of people getting seasick and being very uncomfortable during extended sea voyages. The Channel was somewhat choppy and we soon felt the motion of a boat crossing unstable waters. I got a queasy stomach and feared that Neptune would exact his tribute, but after an uneasy night not in a bunk but in a hammock (the sleeping accommodation for most of the passengers) by morning my stomach had adjusted, and I enjoyed breakfast in the mess hall. In the seven day voyage that followed, the Atlantic was really turbulent at times and the ship dipped and rolled almost like a submarine. Before long most of the passengers kept to their hammocks or bunks and were not often seen in the mess hall for meals. My parents, who were quartered in a different section of the ship, also felt the effects of the stormy ocean but managed fairly well by resting much of the time.

I moved around freely, though always with a small brown paper bag in my pocket just in case. I reported to the two civilian escort officers, a woman and a man, both of whom were Dutch, for my work assignment. We conversed either in English or sometimes in

German. Together with a young Ukrainian, with whom I became friends, I was assigned the task of checking passengers' documents to ensure that all necessary papers were in order for landing in New York. This was not difficult work but kept the Ukrainian and me occupied for most of the voyage. The food on board ship was American military cuisine and included many items served in normal American fast food restaurants. One new item for me was the grapefruit. I considered it practically inedible but a fellow passenger quickly identified it for me in German, "Pampelmuse," and also happily took it off my hands in exchange for an orange. Later I came to like it once I learned to put sugar on it.

Arrival in the United States

Fortunately for all passengers, the last two days of our voyage were much calmer than the stormy early days. In the late afternoon of Saturday, March 1, the S.S. General Taylor, a name that we were instructed to remember for later documentation, approached the New York harbor. We were not allowed to enter the harbor since immigration processing could only be done in the morning of the following day. The lighted New York skyline in the evening and during the night will always remain my first impression of the North American continent. By now most passengers had recovered from seasickness and appeared quite regularly for meals. The atmosphere became livelier and everyone was anticipating the disembarkation with hope but also some uncertainty. In the early morning the ship sailed slowly into the harbor past the Statue of Liberty and many moving and docked vessels. At last the S.S. General Taylor was secured at a pier and the fairly orderly disembarkation got underway.

Hundreds and hundreds of passengers filled the large hall on the pier in slow, long lines of processing. In the far end of the hall we could see a much smaller group of people, cordoned off from the arriving passengers, who were anticipating the newly arrived. After passing most of the checkpoints, my dad told me to stay with the hand luggage and he and my mother set off to see if there were any of our relatives among that small group. My father was quite quickly recognized by his cousin Carrie Petukat from Brooklyn and my cousin Art Kasewurm from Westfield, Massachusetts, who, along with his cousin Fred Norwat, began to shout my dad's name. Even though the relatives had not known the name of our ship or the pier at which it was to dock, after some inquiries they had guessed the right place In contrast, the great majority of arriving immigrants were coming to the strange new land of America, often knowing little of the language and were met by strangers to give them directions how to travel to their final destination. We were very fortunate to be met by relatives with whom we had corresponded and a few of whom my father knew personally. This eased the shock of being transplanted into a new unfamiliar land and society.

After completing the last formalities of the processing, we were released. My cousin Art took all of us to Aunt Carrie's home in Brooklyn for a late lunch and early supper. We left Aunt Carrie's house early in the evening with Art and his cousin Fred, who had come to New York to drive my parents and me to Westfield to spend a week with dad's oldest sister Anna Kasewurm, my cousin Art, his wife Doris, and their four young children. We also met relatives on the Kasewurm side of the family living in the Westfield area. I recognized some of them from the names in letters from my Aunt Anna. Also several of them had sent gift packages to my parents and to some of the other relatives in Germany during the difficult years immediately after the war. Fortunately for my parents, all the older relatives still spoke German so there was no problem communicating with them. I myself was quite happy to be immersed in English-speaking company to expand my command of the language. In Westfield I also saw the first TV in my life, since it was either very rare or nonexistent in Germany at that time.

After a week in Massachusetts, Art's cousin Ed Norwat took us back to Brooklyn, where we spent a full week with Aunt Carrie Petukat. This cousin of my dad had generously supported us with gift parcels when we needed them very badly in 1946 and early 1947. We could now thank her and all the other relatives personally for the help they had extended to us during those difficult times. I had read about New York and would have liked to have seen more sights there, but that did not happen until decades later. Aunt Carrie was devoutly religious, belonging to a Pentecostal congregation, so we also attended at least two prayer meetings at her church. It was at these prayer meetings that I observed for the only time in my life people "speaking in tongues" (glossolalia), uttering incomprehensible sounds supposedly of divine inspiration. More meaningful for my parents and me was a visit with Dr. George Simons, my dad's former district superintendent in Lithuania in the early twenties and influential American missionary in the Baltic region before the First World War. In his seventies, Dr. Simons was still serving a church in Glendale, New York City. He was surprised and happy to see us. His German was still excellent and he remembered well the years in the Baltic region before the First World War under Russian rule and afterwards as independent states. He was succeeded by Bishop Raymond J. Wade when the former Slavic Mission Conference was placed under an independent American bishop stationed in Stockholm. The Sunday after our midweek visit we attended Dr. Simons' church service. He immediately invited my father to give the sermon, which he translated into English for his congregation. It was to be the first and last formal sermon that my father gave after leaving Germany.

After the week in New York, we boarded a train for our journey to Minneapolis, our final destination. Aunt Emilie Fischer eagerly awaited our arrival and graciously took us into her home, which she shared with my parents for the next two years. I also stayed there during the summer months when I was not attending college. One of my unforgettable memories of Minneapolis is the historic snowstorm around April 1, 1952, which blanketed the region with mountains of snow and was followed by huge floods when the snow melted. We had not seen such masses of snow since before the Second World War in Lithuania.

For my parents and me America was a new world but not so different from Europe or difficult to get used to, except that my parents had to learn a new language. We noticed the great abundance of goods and commodities and encountered attitudes and practices that were new to us. For me communication was not a problem, since I spoke the language well enough to be able to converse on everyday subjects. What I had to learn were typical American idioms and slang words and to expand my overall vocabulary. It was more difficult for my parents, who were much older than I, and had had only very little exposure to English. With several years of evening school and exposure to English in everyday life they gradually acquired a functional use of the language. My mother enjoyed watching some TV programs, which also improved her language skills more quickly. Years later she came to speak and write English quite well.

It was not realistic for my father to return to the church ministry, even though he had hoped that this might be possible some day. He was in his early sixties, and the lack of fluent English closed that door for him. After half a year he found a job as a shipping clerk in a Minneapolis fabric store, where Aunt Emilie's late husband Adam, a tailor, had had business contacts. My dad's small earnings qualified him for Social Security benefits after a little over three years; he continued to work part time at his job until 1966 when failing eyesight forced him to retire at age 76. From the very start, Aunt Emilie proposed that I go to college rather than seek full time work. She was very generous in helping support my parents for a while, so I was able to continue my formal education. Otherwise I would have been drafted soon after registering with a draft board, as I was required to do within six months after my arrival in the States. I was twenty years old and was called up for my first physical examination within two months after registering and passed it without reservation. No doubt, induction would have followed, but I had already entered college. I was given a one-semester deferment, which was then renewed throughout my college and graduate school years. My continuing deferment was most likely possible because the draft board district in Minneapolis in which I was registered had a large enough pool of draft eligible young men to meet its quota, sparing some of us who were college and graduate students. I avoided taking the Selective Service Test, for I feared that my lack of familiarity with American tests would unfavorably affect my testing score. Fortunately, my draft board deferred me solely on the basis of my college grades, which I had to submit at the end of every semester and later at the end of every academic year.

References

Divine, Robert A. *American Immigration Policy, 1924-1952.* New Haven: Yale University Press, 1957.

Holleuffer, Henriette von. *Zwischen Fremde und Fremde: Displaced Persons in Australien, den USA und Kanada 1946-1952.* Osnabrück: Universitätsverlag Rasch, 2001.

Loescher, Gil, and John A. Scanlan. *Calculated Kindness: Refugees and America's Half-Open Door 1945 to the Present.* New York and London: The Free Press, 1986.

Epilogue

My life in the United States has not been so unique to warrant more than a short summary. Soon after we arrived in Minneapolis, I was anxious to find out my chances of continuing my education in an American college, since I was one year shy of obtaining a high school diploma or Abitur from the Oberrealschule in Schwäbisch Hall, Germany. While still in Germany I had learned enough about the American secondary school and college systems to know that with my incomplete German secondary education I should be able to continue possibly even as a college sophomore. German academic high school graduates were accepted as beginning juniors in some American colleges because German academic secondary schools required a year or two longer than American high schools. A friend of Aunt Emilie, an engineering professor at the University of Minnesota, was happy to introduce me at the office of foreign students. A not very friendly lady looked over my high school record and then expressed doubt that I would be able to enter the University as a beginning college student. She was not familiar with rigorous German high schools where my B average was a respectable achievement. She suggested two choices: one to attend an American high school and obtain a diploma or to take some summer school courses to see whether I could do college level work. At first, this was disappointing for I certainly had no desire to go back to high school as a twenty- year-old, and the second option, though practical, was not particularly appealing either.

Fortunately Aunt Emilie had another suggestion. The pastor of the Methodist Church that she attended was a member of the Hamline University Board of Trustees, and she arranged to have him introduce me at Hamline. He took me to the Director of Admissions, Dr.

Arthur Williamson, who was also a history professor, and quite importantly, had recently returned from a sabbatical in Europe, where he had familiarized himself with secondary education systems. Dr. Williamson thought I would have no major problems doing college level work, since my command of English was quite good and my German high school record acceptable. He proposed that I be admitted as a special student at Hamline University first and then be reclassified as a regular student at the end of the academic year. Since Hamline was already in the middle of the spring semester, I would be admitted for the fall semester. In addition, he suggested that I spend the first semester as a student on campus rather than commute from home in order to find my way more quickly into the American college milieu. This was excellent advice. I liked living on campus so well that I stayed there throughout my four years in college.

Several weeks after my visit to the Hamline campus I received a letter, notifying me of my admission for the fall semester and a full tuition scholarship award for the first year. This was more than I expected, and I remain grateful to Hamline for the confidence placed in me at a critical time in my life. As it was, I earned either full or half tuition scholarships for the other three years at Hamline based on my academic record. In those days, it was still possible for students to work their way through college without falling behind in normal four-year progress towards an undergraduate degree thereby avoiding major debts. Starting in my sophomore year my part time work on campus during the year paid enough to cover room and board in a dormitory. My summer earnings in various kinds of jobs, from work in a battery manufacturing plant to maintenance and painting of houses, enabled me to pay for the part of my tuition that scholarships after my sophomore year did not cover.

I started out with a light academic load but soon discovered that I could readily keep pace with my American peers. The demanding curriculum of the German academic secondary schools with three mandatory foreign languages, advanced mathematics, science, and humanities courses had prepared me very well for the challenges of American college. I was especially happy that I would no longer have to contend with advanced mathematics but could now concentrate on literature, history, political science, sociology, psychology, economics, and philosophy. In order to become familiar with the English terminology in science and to fulfill some general education requirements, I elected a semester course in general biology in the first semester of my freshman year, which was excellently taught. A follow-up course gave me a broad overview of the other natural sciences. For a major, at first I leaned toward foreign languages, German and French, but then turned toward history as my special interest. In my choice of history courses I intentionally emphasized American history in order to become better grounded in the past (and present) of my new homeland. As for a future profession, secondary school teaching seemed to be an appealing option, since it would enable me to continue pursuing my intellectual interests and the fairly rapidly growing population of the United States promised many job openings for new secondary school teachers. However early in my sophomore year several of my professors suggested college teaching as a more suitable career option for me. I still wanted to prepare for secondary school teaching as a backup, knowing that I would face many years of graduate work while getting ready for college teaching and might have to interrupt my education to earn support to continue.

I enjoyed some of the required education courses for high school teaching, but began to have doubts about practice teaching projected for my senior year. Advice from one of my political science professors, Scott Johnston, during my junior year not to "waste my time" taking education courses but to concentrate on solid disciplinary subjects persuaded me to drop out of teacher training – with considerable relief. I was now able to develop a second, though unofficial major, in political science. In addition, I felt freer to continue my participation in several campus organizations.

As I started exploring graduate schools and graduate fellowship programs offered by history departments, I discovered that there were very few departmental awards available during the first year of graduate study. Teaching or research assistantships were the most common awards, but they were generally not open to entering graduate students. Fortunately, the growing national demand for college teachers in the later 1950s led to the establishment of the national Woodrow Wilson Fellowship, which supported the first year of graduate study, and the Danforth Graduate Fellowship, which covered the full graduate student's program. Two of my fellow seniors and I were nominated for the national Danforth Graduate Fellowship competition from Hamline. I might not even have heard of the national fellowship programs if I had attended the large University of Minnesota. A small liberal arts institution like Hamline offered significant advantages in preparing for national competitions. It was not only high grades that counted but also active participation in campus life and organizations. Very critical was having professors who came to know individual students well. Perhaps to the surprise of the college, all three of us received awards of the 77 in the nation, which enabled us to pursue graduate study without financial worries. During the interview for the Danforth Graduate Fellowship I was questioned closely why I chose the University of Minnesota for graduate work in German history, since there were other outstanding graduate programs in the nation. I must have offered enough convincing educational reasons for my preferred choice, even though a very important consideration, which I did not dare mention, was that I could live at home and thereby help my parents financially. However, I never regretted having chosen the University of Minnesota because its broad requirements for the history Ph.D. enabled me to satisfy my intellectual interests in different areas of history and even outside of history in political science and world geography. This kind of training prepared me better for teaching in a liberal arts college than the more narrowly focused graduate history programs at most other universities would have done.

Most important for my life was that I met my life partner through Hamline and the University of Minnesota. Beverly was a freshman at Hamline when I was already a senior there. We did not have any classes together but both of us met in the women's dining room and kitchen, where she worked as a waitress and I was a dishwasher. No romantic interest ensued from that encounter. However, since I briefly dated her roommate, she probably knew more about me than I may have realized. Only four years later when we both were graduate students at the University of Minnesota, where she majored in anatomy, we happened to have carrels on the same level of the University library and a chance encounter in the fall of 1960 sparked a relationship that led to marriage in early September 1961. We decided that we could make it financially on the research award that she held and my part time instructorship to start life together even before we had completed our graduate degrees. During our last year at the University we occupied a rather nice basement apartment near the campus, while preparing our theses. Beverly had progressed to some doctoral work in anatomy but elected to finish with a master's degree. I spent most of the year writing my doctoral dissertation and teaching half time. Coincidentally, we ended up having our final orals for our degrees on the very same day and during the very same hours in July 1962.

At the time we were completing our academic work at Minnesota, we already knew that we were headed for Stockton, California, for our first jobs. My job hunt had resulted in an appointment at an innovative academic three-year liberal arts college, Raymond College, to be opened at the University of the Pacific in early September 1962. While interviewing for my job, I also talked to the placement officer of the Stockton Unified School District about a position for Beverly in a high school. Since she was trained as an undergraduate to teach biology and mathematics, her qualifications were of immediate interest. She was offered a position at Stagg High School in Stockton, where she taught mostly chemistry and biology during her first and only year of secondary school teaching. When we moved to Stockton in late August 1962, we did not anticipate that it would become our permanent city of residence where I was to spend 37 years of association with the University of the Pacific until my retirement. Beverly found very successful careers in helping establish and then leading a Planned Parenthood affiliate in Stockton for almost twenty years. After retiring from that, she helped organize Solar Cookers International in Sacramento, which she directed for fourteen years. She has done a marvelous job not only as a highly accomplished professional but also as a devoted mother to our twins, Barbara and Alfred, born in 1964. They in turn have become successful professionals in their own right and delightful people. After college Barbara served two years in the Peace Corps in Lesotho, and then obtained her Ph.D. in biomedical engineering. She oversees research at an orthopedic company and also runs marathons. Alfred, a licenced civil engineer, is with the California Department of Transportation. In addition, he earned a second degree, in history, his favorite avocation. He and his lovely wife Julienne, an accomplished professional in theatre costuming, presented us with our first grandchild, Gabriel, in June 2004, and a second, Avery, in August 2006.

Leaving Minneapolis after a record setting cold winter for (not always sunny) northern California had been rather easy for us. My parents and Beverly's widowed mother found our departure less easy but accepted it. In 1954, my parents had bought, with Aunt Emilie's help, a narrow duplex in north Minneapolis, in which they occupied one apartment and rented out the other for income to help retire the mortgage. My father continued to work first full time and then part

time until 1966, when diminished eyesight forced his retirement.
Beverly's mother carried on with her employment at the University
of Minnesota until her retirement several years later. She came to
visit us repeatedly and eventually moved to Stockton permanently
in 1967, and even remarried. Six years after my father's death in
1970 my mother gave up her home in Minneapolis and moved to
Stockton, where she lived until her death in 1983. Three years later
Beverly's mother also died. Aunt Emilie sold her property in 1959
and moved into an apartment in a house that a cousin of mine acquired whose immigration from Germany she had sponsored, four
years after my parents and I arrived. Years later, when my cousin
and his wife decided to leave Minneapolis and to move to southern
California, Aunt Emilie went into the Walker Methodist Retirement
Home in Minneapolis, where she died in 1977.

Looking back upon my years in Europe and the United States, I
am impressed how fortunate I was to survive the war years in Eastern Europe and central Germany and to find a normal life in the
United States. Niccolò Machiavelli, the cynical political sage of the
Renaissance, remarked that humans control over half of their fate,
the rest was given to fortune and chance. Even though an individual's drive and motivation are critical to the achievement of a quality
life, circumstances and the presence of certain persons and human
associations are essential to the realization of a full life. My parents
and I were lucky to escape from Soviet-occupied eastern and central
Germany with the help of acquaintances and strangers, where at the
time deportations for labor within Germany or to the waste lands
of the Soviet Union remained an everyday threat. We also had not
suffered any undue physical and mental harm during the war and its
immediate aftermath. Once we crossed the Iron Curtain, we were
more secure and had reached a part of Germany that was gradually reviving from the devastating war and its painful aftermath. My
dad's association with the Methodist church eased his return to a

livelihood that sustained us during our years in West Germany. Of foremost importance in our life's journey was having a circle of relatives who had escaped to West Germany earlier, and another smaller group who had immigrated to the United States before World War I and had become established there with their own extended families. Our German relatives enabled us to gain a foothold in then American-occupied Bavaria and several of our American relatives helped us during the postwar time of severe shortages of food and basic necessities in Germany. Among my American relatives my Aunt Emilie Fischer stands out as the great pillar of very generous support of my family and several other relatives in West Germany immediately after the war. Several years later, in 1951-52, she also was the key sponsor who made it possible for my parents and me to cross the Atlantic Ocean and to start a new life in Minnesota.

Printed in the United States
by Baker & Taylor Publisher Services